CREATING PLACES - THE PODCAST TRANSCRIPTS

THE ART OF WORLD BUILDING

VOLUME V

RANDY ELLEFSON

Evermore Press
GAITHERSBURG, MARYLAND

Evermore Press, LLC
Gaithersburg, Maryland
www.evermorepress.org

Publisher's Note: This book includes fictional passages. All names, characters, locations, and incidents are products of the author's imagination, or have been used fictitiously. Any semblance to actual persons living or dead, locales, or events is coincidental and not intended by the author.

Creating Places – The Podcast Transcripts / Randy Ellefson. -- 1st ed.
ISBN 978-1-946995-16-2 (Amazon paperback)
ISBN 978-1-946995-19-3 (IngramSpark paperback)
ISBN 978-1-946995-17-9 (IngramSpark hardcover)

CONTENTS

ACKNOWLEDGEMENTS

Cover design by Deranged Doctor Designs

FOREWORD

This collection of transcripts from *The Art of World Building Podcast* is based on a series of non-fiction books, *The Art of World Building*. That series is divided into three volumes. The second is *Creating Places*. Each episode is based on a chapter (or part of one) from that book, with additional information and tips not found there.

These transcripts are designed for the podcast listeners (and anyone else who wants them) to have a written copy of the episodes to take with them anywhere and not need an internet connection. They are casual in presentation and unedited, except that each episode features section breaks with music and voiceovers; the latter have been removed from these transcripts and placed in the appendix to avoid repetition.

HOW TO
CREATE PLANETS

Hello and welcome *to The Art of World Build-ing Podcast*, episode number eleven, part 1. Today's topic is about how to create a planet. This includes talking about its rotation, other planets in the solar system, aster-oids, comets, constellations, and the impact of the Sun and moon on tides, hours in the days, and seasons. This materi-al and more is discussed in chapter 2 of *Creating Places*, volume 2 in *The Art of World Building* book series.

BASICS ON PLANETS

In an earlier episode, I may have mentioned this idea that we talk about world building, but we don't normally invent the entire planet. However, that is the subject of this par-ticular episode. When I say that we don't normally create the entire planet, I mean that we don't do so in extreme detail. We usually just pick a region or maybe one conti-nent. So, in this episode when we talk about creating a planet, we're not talking about doing the entire thing in detail, meaning every last civilization. We're talking about the actual planet itself.

We may only develop one area of it extensively, but we still need the actual planet, of course. The focus of this episode is not just a planet, but one that is relatively similar to Earth. And the reason for this is that this is what most of us are probably going to invent. Even if we have unusual planets, our characters are probably coming from one that is more Earth-like. So, what I'm not going to cover in this episode is any planet where the physics are dramatically different. This includes ideas like gravity being wildly different or the planet being tidally locked to its Sun.

These are certainly good ideas to explore, but one reason I'm going to not focus on this is that, for one, most of us do need an Earth-like setting – at least one of them – but there are so many variations that we could do, and some of them are found in nature, that I can't possibly cover them all. I'm also not a physicist or an astronomer, so if you're looking for information on oddball planets, unfortunately, that's not what we're going to cover today.

Such planets are probably more useful to those who are writing science fiction than fantasy, but there's no reason that we can't have fantasy characters who are hopping from one planet to another the same way that we do in science fiction. It's just that in sci-fi we use a ship, and in a fantasy setting we would probably use something like a magic portal.

Worlds that are not Earth-like are good places for our characters to visit temporarily. And one reason we might want to do that is if there is something valuable on that planet. Any planet that is markedly different from Earth is probably going to have limited use to us as well. That might also be true of our characters. Regardless, we're going to focus on an Earth-like world. So, here we go.

ROTATION

The first thing we should talk about is rotation. Because, on a planet like Earth, the planet is spinning one direction or the other. It's either counterclockwise or clockwise. Which direction are we going? Counterclockwise. And this is why the Sun rises in the east and sets in the west. If you want to do something different, you can decide that your planet is spinning the other direction and, therefore, these are reversed. This is a really quick way to pull your audience out of their comfort zone. This also means that other celestial bodies are also rotating in the opposite direction.

Whether this has a practical impact on your world is debatable because, for most of us, we're probably not going to be talking much about this. One on hand, this seems like a big change, but it doesn't really change much about the details of the world. In other words, this alone is not going to make it stop being Earth-like.

Now, there are some basic things that are affected, and we're going to talk a little bit more about this later. One of them is the ocean currents, and another one is which coast of a continent has warmer or colder air. Another issue is the way the prevailing winds will be reversed in each hemisphere. And if you're wondering what I'm talking about with all of those, we're going to dive a little bit more into that in a few minutes.

The good news is that all of these impacts are simply a matter of reversing a direction that I'm going to talk about later. For example, if the planet is rotating one way and that causes warm water to be on one coast, and then you decide it's rotating the other way, you just have to decide it's on the opposite coast. I wanted to mention that now just in case I forget to mention it later when we're talking about some of those issues. It's just a matter of reversal.

THE SUN'S IMPACT

The next thing I want to talk about is the impact of the Sun. You may have heard of this idea of a Goldilocks Zone. And what that means is that our planet is not too close and not too far away from the Sun for life to occur. Most of us are going to want to just leave this issue alone and not touch it. If you're entertaining the idea of having the Sun be larger in the sky, that could mean one of two things: Either the planet is much closer to it and not in the habitable zone, or the sun itself is much larger than our Sun is.

This issue of size could be a problem because it's possible that this means the Sun is putting out more radiation or that the solar wind from that Sun is significantly stronger. And this is the kind of area that I don't want to get into too much because, again, I'm not an astronomer and I don't want to give you misinformation. But this is one of the reasons why we're focused on an Earth-like world.

We could also decide to do a different kind of sun, such as a red dwarf. Such a sun has a smaller habitable zone, and it's closer to the actual sun. This means, of course, that the planet is that close to the sun, and this has a side-effect known as tidal locking. This has nothing to do with tides and oceans. What it means is that the same side of the planet is always facing the sun, and what that means is that one side is basically being blasted with sunlight all the time, and the other side is in perpetual darkness.

Now, on one hand this sounds kind of cool, but on the other hand one side is not going to be habitable because it's too hot, and the other side is going to be too cold. So, we're probably talking about a planet that is not Earth-like, and therefore it's not the subject of this episode. But, I don't want to discourage you from exploring these options for planets that our characters visit temporarily.

THE MOON'S IMPACT

The next thing to talk about is the impact of the Moon, and this is a big subject. It includes tidal locking, tides, the seasons, the hours in the day, and, of course, moonlight. Let's talk a little bit about our own moon and how that contrasts to other moons that we have found in our solar system. This is not a recommendation that your moon be the same, but this will give us a baseline for variations.

Our moon has no atmosphere, but other moons in our solar system sometimes do have one, but it's very toxic. Our moon also has no volcanic activity, unlike many of the moons in our solar system. And these are not necessarily unrelated facts. You might also be aware that the planet Mars has no atmosphere. On the other hand, a planet like Venus does. And, of course, so do we. So, one question is why is this the case? And what I'm about to tell you is true whether we're talking about a planet or a moon.

Basically, what scientists have said is that if there is internal activity going on within the planet, the kind of activity that results in volcanoes, this has a side-effect of creating magnetism. This magnetism matters because it stretches out far from the body and turns into a kind of shield that protects the body from the solar wind that is coming off of the sun. If this magnetic shield is not there, then the sun's solar wind literally blows away the planet or the moon's atmosphere. It's been speculated that this is the reason why Mars no longer has an atmosphere. It's believed that it once did, and we've seen evidence of things like rivers on the surface.

So then, that begs the question, well, where did the water go and what happened to the atmosphere? The last I heard, there is no longer any geologic activity on Mars, and, as a result, the magnetic shield is gone and, as a result of that, the solar wind blew away its atmosphere and now it's a dead planet. This may be what happened to our moon, but it doesn't really matter what happened to our moon. This is the basic idea.

Part of what I'm telling you here is that if you'd like to have a moon that has an atmosphere and forests and the whole bit just like we have here on Earth, you can do this. And we'll talk a little bit more about this as we go along.

Another issue regarding the moon is that our moon is relatively large compared to the planet that it is orbiting. Most of them that we've found in our solar system, and even in other solar systems, are significantly smaller. Why does this matter? Well, you should just understand the size of our moon because if you decide to make one that's much bigger than ours, it's going to have a bigger impact on the planet.

It is arguable more likely that, in a fictional world and a fictional moon, that it's actually going to be smaller than ours. However, by doing so, you are going to change its impact. And we're going to talk about what would happen if you did this.

Another basic factor to consider about our moon is that it is in a relatively stable orbit. It is mostly circular, but a lot of moons out there are more elliptical. It's more like an oval. The basic issue that this is going to cause is that when the moon is closer to the planet it's going to have more impact on it, and when it's further away it's going to have less. Again, most of us are going to want to go with something Earth-like and be done with it.

Another basic fact to consider is that almost every body in a solar system is going to be rotating the same direction. This is caused by the gravity that caused everything to form in the first place. Basically, what happens as a solar system is forming is that all the dust out there is swirling, or it starts to swirl. As it gets closer to each other and it starts to clump together, it starts to form these masses. Because everything is spinning, it's all spinning in the same direction.

Now, it is possible to have a moon or even a planet that is orbiting something in the opposite direction, but usually what this means is that that body formed somewhere else and was captured by the gravity of the thing that it is now orbiting. Generally, the larger moons are orbiting in the same direction, and some of the smaller ones are the ones that are going backwards or retrograde.

If you're interested in more than one moon around your planet, go with one main one that is more like ours, and then a second one. And this second one would be smaller, further away, and have this retrograde motion if you wanted it to. If you're wondering how a moon could possibly be captured like this, as it turns out, celestial bodies are not always staying in their orbit. In fact, more recent research has shown that Jupiter has been responsible for all sorts of things happening with planets changing their orbits. And, sometimes, what happens is a planet or a moon gets flung out of its orbit and out of a solar system, and it could just end up going across empty space for eternity. But, sometimes, it might end up going into another solar system somewhere, or even another galaxy eventually, and getting caught in another gravitational pull.

TIDAL LOCKING

Let's talk about something I mentioned earlier: tidal locking. If you've ever wondered why the same side of the moon is always facing us, the answer is tidal locking. This means that the moon rotates in the same number of days that it takes to orbit us. When I first heard of this, I thought it was pretty coincidental in that it's probably rare. Well, the reality is this is what's going to happen to pretty much everything eventually, and the reason is gravity.

Despite the huge distances that often separate bodies in space, they effect each other, and that effect is generally one of gravity. Gravity causes objects to either speed up in the case of something that has an elliptical orbit, or to slow down. And that can also happen with an elliptical orbit when it's further away from the body that it is orbiting.

Tidal locking is an eventual result that is caused by this gravity. The moons that are closest to a planet are the first to be tidally locked. So, if you decide to do this and you've got three moons, don't make the first one still be spinning and the second one be tidally locked because that doesn't make any sense. Actually, there is one potential scenario where that could work, and that would be if the closer moon was recently captured. I can't stress enough that tidal locking is an eventual result. Even our own planet,

If given the time, is going to eventually be tidally locked to the Sun. It's also possible for both bodies to be tidally locked to each other. For example, in the case of the Earth, it is only the Moon that is tidally locked to us. If we were to stand on the Moon looking at the Earth, we would still see the Earth spinning, so we would not always see the same side of the Earth. If only one of the two bodies is tidally locked, it's always going to be the smaller one. In other words, it's going to be the moon.

One really interesting scenario about a moon and a planet that are both tidally locked to each other is that if this was the case and you were standing on the surface of the Earth, for example, the Moon would always be in the exact same spot in the sky. It would not be rising and falling like the Sun. It would literally never move. One of the reasons that this is interesting is that half of the planet would see it, and the other half wouldn't and would have no idea that it even existed unless people wrote about it or there was enough technology to get around to the other side of the planet.

What if you have a typical fantasy world where the only way to travel is either by dragon or by taking a ship, and you travel around the side of the world, you go across a big ocean and, the next thing you know, there's this big thing hanging out there in the sky and it's always there? You're probably going to wondering, "What is that?"

This would have a big effect on the tides, as well, because the Moon is mostly responsible for tides. And tides are the next subject we're going to discuss.

TIDES

If we want to have a different number of moons than we have her on Earth, we need to understand the moon's effect on the tides. While coastlines and currents have an effect on the tides, by far the Moon is the biggest impact, followed by the Sun. You may have heard that the Moon and the Earth are actually getting further apart, but this is happening at such a small rate that we're never going to notice. Tides are the reason that this is happening.

The basic idea behind tides is that the Moon is causing a high tide on the side of the Earth that it faces because it is pulling the ocean away from the planet. And, as it turns out, the Moon is also pulling the Earth away from the water that's on the opposite side of the planet, which causes a second high tide there. In the *Creating Places* book and on the website, I have some images that help make this kind of thing clearer. You can just go to artofworldbuilding.com and, on the menu for the second volume, there's a link for images. And then, once you get to that page, the images for this particular episode would be under chapter 2.

The quick takeaway here is that the Moon causes high tide on opposite sides of the planet, and on the other two sides of the planet, those experience low tide at the same time. This means that there are two high tides and two low tides every day. The two high tides are not going to be the same height, however.

For most world builders, this is only really going to matter if you decide to have a moon with an elliptical orbit, because when it's further away from the planet, the effect on the tides is going to be lower. By contrast, when it's closer, it's going to have more effect. This is just something to be aware of before you decide that your moon has an elliptical orbit and you never give it a second thought. This is a consequence of that.

Another issue affecting the height of the tides is that sometimes the Moon and the Sun are on the same side of the planet and that is going to cause the highest tides on that side. Another factor affecting the height of the tides is the mass and distance of the moon from the planet. The moon's diameter, or its apparent size in the sky, has nothing to do with it. If we were to change the distance of the moon from the planet, or the mass of it, it's going to change the effect it has on the planet. Fortunately, no one's expecting us to tell them the mass of our moons or the distance, and, not to mention, how those compare to the one we have here on Earth, so we can largely ignore this. But I'm just going to throw it out there as an FYI.

Now, one thing that I'm sure you're very curious about is what happens if we add a second moon to a planet. I go into a lot of detail in chapter 2 of *Creating Places*, but the short answer is that just like when the Moon and the Sun are on the same side of the planet, if you have two moons and they're on the same side of the planet, they're going to be pulling more on that side and causing a higher tide.

HOURS IN THE DAY

It may surprise you to know that the Moon is partly responsible for us having 24-hour days. Both the Moon and the Earth are spinning slower and slower. The reason is that their gravity is affecting each other. And, in the case of the Moon, it is causing the Earth to spin slower, and this is causing the days to get longer. A billion years ago, we had much shorter days. Why? Well, because we were spinning faster. If you have always wanted there to be another hour in the day, then I suggest coming back in 100,000 or 200,000 years, and you will get your wish. Of course, that doesn't mean you're actually going to live any longer.

If we want a scenario where our planet has very short days, then we could decide that there is no moon and, therefore, this slowing has never taken place. However, the lack of a moon will cause other problems. One of those would be a lack of stronger tides, and then there is the fact that the Moon is helping stabilize the tilt of the Earth. And, therefore, that's affecting the seasons, which we're going to talk about in a minute.

THE SEASONS

Actually, let's do it now. So, the Moon is stabilizing the Earth's tilt. The Earth is basically leaned over a certain amount – roughly 23.5 degrees. This means that as we rotate around the Sun, one pole is facing toward the Sun and the other one is facing away. In other words, what this gives us is the seasons. So, if you take away the Moon and now the Earth is wobbling chaotically, then there aren't going to be any seasons. Basically, if the Moon went away or was destroyed by some sort of asteroid strike, that would be it for the Earth. Maybe not directly, but sooner or later all life on Earth would end up dying because of the Moon being gone.

Even worse, the Moon is helping to stabilize the Earth's orbit around the Sun so that we have a roughly circular orbit. And, without the Moon, that would also destabilize, and we would end up with an elliptical orbit, which means, at times, we would be too hot, and, other times, too cold.

The last thing about the Moon and its effect on the planet is moonlight, of course. If you don't have a moon, you don't have any moonlight. Another issue is that the reason we get moonlight is that our moon is barren, and, therefore, reflects the Sun. if you decided to create a moon that has an atmosphere and a forest and oceans and all that, that is not going to be nearly as reflective. And so, therefore, any moonlight that is shining down on the planet is going to be considerably muted. It would probably be a mistake to have a forested moon and then talk about the characters on the planet being out in bright moonlight.

STARS, CONSTELLATIONS, AND OTHER PLANETS

Let's conclude by talking about some other things that our inhabitants on our planet would see if they look out into the sky, such as stars, constellations, asteroids, comets, and, of course, other planets in the solar system. If we're doing fantasy, we may think that we have no need of these. And, in fact, we may not. But, sometimes it can be interesting to add them and help create a sense of a wider world. They don't take that much effort to do, either.

When it comes to other planets, you should be aware that rocky planets, like Mercury, Venus and Earth – and even Mars – are closer to the Sun, while the gas and ice giants are going to be further away. Now, when I first did some research on that, that was assumed to be the case. But some of the more recent discoveries by scientists has suggested that something like a gas giant can actually be close to the sun. I think the jury is still out on whether they form there or not, because there are competing theories about what's gone on in the formation of our solar system. But one thing that we do know for sure at this point, as far as the scientists have said, is that planets can migrate and change their place within the solar system. In ours, the big culprit behind this is actually Jupiter because it has the biggest mass of anything else besides the Sun.

There is something known as a "hot Jupiter," and what these are are giant gas planets, just like Jupiter, but they are very close to the Sun – even closer than Mercury. Now, it might sound like I'm giving you some conflicted information, and, in a way, I am, but that's because of new discoveries have changed things. So, what you should do here is just generally follow the advice that rocky planets are closer and that the gas giants and ice giants are further away. But, if you want to mix this up a little bit, you can probably get away with it. Just be aware that, depending on what someone else knows in your audience, they may decide that you're wrong, you don't know what you're talking about. But there is some flexibility here.

Also, be aware that Saturn is not the only planet in our system that has rings. Some of the others have them as well, but they are harder to see, partly because they may be made of darker materials. The ones around Saturn are mostly ice, and that's why we can see them.

Earlier, I mentioned the idea of a habitable or Goldi-locks Zone where planets can be, and life can flourish on those planets. Again, at last check, scientists have decided that only two or three planets can exist within that zone if the star is a yellow star like ours. There just isn't room for more than that.

CONSTELLATIONS

Let's talk a little bit about constellations, which is nothing more than a group of stars that suggests an outline of a person or an object. Since things are rotating the stars and, therefore, constellations that are visible in the sky change. Here on Earth, and in a fantasy setting, we may have as-signed supernatural elements to some of these constella-tions, but this could also happen in science fiction even if people no longer believe in that sort of thing. And on Earth, many of us don't believe in them. Well, we believe in the constellation, but whatever it was supposed to sym-bolize is something we don't necessarily ascribe to.

One great thing about constellations is that we can just invent this and there doesn't need to be any explanation for it. Something to consider is whether or not a constella-tion is near the equator or not. If so, then it doesn't matter whether you are in the northern or southern hemisphere, you're going to be able to see it. However, it will appear upside down to you if you're in one versus the other. If the constellation is further towards one of the poles, like the north pole, then people in the southern hemisphere are never going to see that.

In *Creating Places*, I go into a little bit more detail about issues that we could have with constellations, such as having a winter god have a constellation that is further north, but then the other side of the planet can never see that.

If you live in the northern hemisphere then you may be generally unaware of something known as a dark constellation, because most of these appear in the southern hemisphere. A dark constellation is made out of interstellar gas, and it causes a shape in the sky, kind of like when you look up at clouds and see familiar shapes. And the reason we can see this is partly that they are illuminated by stars, and they are also blocking the light of other stars.

If you remember from a previous episode on creating gods, sometimes people talk about good gods versus evil gods. And we could use that to some effect here, deciding that the good gods are the ones that have constellations made out of stars, and the evil gods are the ones that have these dark constellations.

ASTEROIDS AND COMETS

I want to conclude today with a brief mention of passing asteroids and comets. The difference between them is their composition, with the asteroids not having a whole lot of ice, and, therefore, they don't have a tail. The comets do have a certain amount of ice, and then they end up with the tail when they come closer to the sun, which heats up and then melts that ice which forms the tail. Aside from this, we can treat them the same.

The only reason we are likely to care about this is if they come close to our planet. One way that you could use this is for it to strike the planet in the context of your story. And the other way is for it to come by at regular intervals, and that this becomes a momentous occasion that people look forward to. And this has often been used for something like prophecies in fantasy. We can use these to create myths, including the doomsday one.

Make sure you tune in for the next episode when we go into great detail about climates, which is a much more interesting subject than you might think.

How to Create Planets

Hello and welcome *to The Art of World Building Podcast*, episode number eleven, part 2. Today's topic concludes our talk about how to create a planet and focuses on climates. This includes understanding the role of the equator and oceans, climate zones, prevailing winds, rain shadows, and of course the climates themselves. This material and more is discussed in chapter 2 of *Creating Places*, volume 2 in *The Art of World Building* book series.

BASICS ON CLIMATE

Climate is one of those subjects that most of us probably don't find very interesting, but I think that's partly because most of us don't really understand it. I mean, we have a basic understanding just from living on the planet, but we don't really understand the details of it that actually do make it interesting, and we certainly don't understand how those apply to a world that we are inventing. So, by the time we're done with this podcast episode, I think you will find it more interesting that you do right now – or, at least, that's my hope.

When it comes to climate, there are things that affect the entire planet's climate, and then there are things that are happening on a more regional level. So, first, we're going to talk about that bigger picture, and the two primary things we want to focus on are the equator's role and then the role of the ocean.

THE EQUATOR

Let's first talk about the equator. We all know what one is, but it's basically an imaginary line. You know, it doesn't actually exist. It's just a line that's equally distant between the north pole and the south pole. One of the things about the equator is that days and nights are exactly at the same length there year round. This changes the farther north or south you go, to the point where it can be night for six months and then day for six months at one of the poles.

It's also perpetually hot there, except in higher altitudes where it's a little bit cooler. As a general rule, things tend to remain the same at the equator, and the equator is sometimes the exception to some of the other climate things that we're going to talk about today. Since things stay the same, one of the things we don't really have at the equator is the normal four seasons that most of us experience. They just don't exist. Well, technically, they do exist, but they're so subtle that they may as well not. If you are building a fantasy world where the characters in that region never leave that area, then they may not even understand the idea of the seasons, the same way that they would have never seen snow.

Now, they do have something instead of the four pronounced seasons, and that is basically a wet season and a dry season. Some places are actually wet all year, but many of them are just wet for something like 200 days a year on Earth. Of course, this means that they are predominantly wet. If you don't like rain, you probably don't want to live near the equator.

And, now, if you're building a world where there are inhabitants who never leave the equator, then they are probably very used to the rain. They probably take it for granted and their culture as likely to have something to do with this abundant rainfall. Life in this area is often based upon the rain. If you are setting a story at the equator, you should take into account that it's probably going to be raining on the characters most of the time. If this is something you don't want in your story, then you might want to move it further from the equator.

For those of us who write science fiction, you may have wondered why space craft on Earth are usually launched from Florida, and the reason is that this is closest to the equator in the United States. The reason this matters is that the escape velocity needed to escape our atmosphere is less at the equator because the planet is spinning faster there. So, if we're building a science fiction planet, we might want to consider this. We may have decided that the propulsion systems on that planet are so powerful that they don't need to worry about this anymore, but it could be more realistic to decide that they do still need to worry about this, and plan our strategy and our books more with that in mind.

One thing you can do is have a kingdom that is near the equator and, therefore, it is in control of the territory on that continent. And there's another kingdom further north, for example, and that kingdom, the northern one, wants to send spaceships into space, but it has a harder time doing so because it's farther from the equator. And this might cause it to try engaging in a war to gain territory that is closer to the equator. So, this is one way in which our research into world building and how the planet works, and just physics, can help us think of a story scenario.

In the previous episode, we talked about the Earth spinning counter-clockwise, which is why the sun is rising in the east and setting in the west. This is important to remember as we continue through this episode, because some of the other issues I'm going to talk about have something to do with which direction the winds are going and that is based on the direction that the planet is spinning, in part. But the reason I mention it right now is that in order for spacecraft to take advantage of this, they have to launch in an easterly direction. So, you could, again, have another scenario where two kingdoms do have territory near the equator, but one of them must launch its spacecraft over the other one to get into space and, as a result, it's very likely to be shot down. Of course, this is assuming that they are enemies.

Personally, I find this kind of detail more interesting, and this is part of what I alluded to at the beginning, where understanding climate and other things about our planet can make the subject of climate more interesting. And, in this case, it can also impact our story and add a nice bit of realism to what we are doing.

Another issue we should talk about when it comes to the equator is that when we are inventing a continent for our world, we should always make an early decision how far from the equator this continent is. This may not seem like it matters at first, but the distance from the equator is going to determine the direction of the prevailing winds, and those are what carry moisture from one place to another, and that moisture can be blocked by mountains. And that is going to cause something that we're going to talk about in a few minutes called "rain shadows." This also causes the location of deserts and forests, so all of this is related to how far from the equator is this landmass.

If you're not sure why any of that matters, by the time we conclude this podcast episode, you will.

THE OCEAN

Now we're going to talk about the ocean and its affect on the climates, which is actually quite significant. If you have a world that has almost no oceans, then the climates are going to be much more stable everywhere. But, as I mentioned in the previous episode, we are focused on creating an Earth-like planet, not one that has so little water. With that in mind, we're going to take a look, now, at how the oceans affect climate.

The first thing to understand is that the ocean absorbs a lot of heat from the sun. It then distributes that heat around the world as the oceans move. If your planet is not rotating, but is tidally locked to the sun, this is not going to happen. But that does not fit our description of an Earth-like world, but I did want to mention that.

Something to be aware of is that the water tends to circulate in certain directions, and what I'm talking about is, you know, we have one ocean that is really the entire planet. But, here on Earth, we call parts of that ocean the Pacific Ocean or the Atlantic Ocean, even though they're really one, giant body of water. But, that aside, the Atlantic Ocean, the water in that area, it spins in a certain direction. And which direction that is has to do with which direction the Earth is spinning.

And, as it turns out, it's also different in the southern hemisphere versus the northern hemisphere. This might sound a little complicated, but it's actually easier than it seems. In fact, all of the oceans in the southern hemisphere are rotating counter-clockwise, whereas the oceans in the northern hemisphere are rotating clockwise. Since many of my listeners are either going to be in the United States or in other English-speaking countries like Europe, I'm going to focus on the Northern Atlantic Ocean as an example.

The Northern Atlantic Ocean, between the United States and the northern coast of Africa and Europe, is spinning clockwise. And this means that warm water from the equator is going up the eastern side of the United States, and, conversely, cold water from near Europe in the northern part of Europe is going down towards the equator along the coast of Africa. And then it goes back west across the equator. So, the ocean is spinning in a giant circle.

They say a picture is worth a thousand words, and it turns out I've got one on the Artofworldbuilding.com website. It's under the *Creating Places* book. There is a page for all the images that are in the book, and it is Figure 14 from Chapter 2. It shows all of the ocean currents on Earth with blue arrows showing where the cold water is going, red arrows showing where the warm water is going, and black arrows showing water that's probably basically in between the two of them.

Even without the picture, it's relatively easy to picture this. If you just imagine the Atlantic Ocean in the north and you're looking at the map, the water on the left side of the ocean is going up, and then it goes across the top to the right, and then it goes down the right side of the ocean, and then back left across the bottom.

So, what does this mean for climate? Well, on the eastern coast of the United States, there is warm water that is going up that coast. And, as a result, this is impacting the climate by bringing warmer and moist air there. The opposite is true on the other side of the United States where the

Pacific Ocean is bringing cold water down from Alaska along the western coast of California and Oregon and Washington State. And, as a result, the water is much colder there. So, as someone who grew up on the eastern United States, I am used to going into the ocean in the summer and having the water being relatively warm. And I have gone to vacation on the western side of the United States and gotten in the water there and been shocked at how cold it is. And this is what's going on.

Now, I did mention the idea that you could decide to have your planet rotating in the opposite direction. You know, the Earth is going counter-clockwise. If you decide to have your planet going clockwise, then that means that all the Earth's ocean direction of the currents that I just talked about will be reversed.

Now, I did mention that in the southern hemisphere the water is swirling in the other direction. But, as it turns out, the affect is the same, and here's what I mean: Regardless of whether you are in the northern or southern hemisphere, the water on the western coast tends to be colder than the water on the eastern coast. It's true regardless of which hemisphere that you are in. The reason this is true is that in the southern hemisphere, the cold water from the pole is being pulled counter-clockwise up the right side of the ocean. Which means, once again, it's on the western edge of a continent. Similarly, since the water is going counter-clockwise, the water from the equator is going down the left side of the ocean, which is the eastern and right side of a continent if we're looking at the map. So, the rule does hold true. Regardless of hemisphere, on Earth or any planet where the world is spinning counter-clockwise, the water on the west coast is colder, and the water on the east coast is warmer.

As we continue our talk about climates, you'll see how this affects everything.

CLIMATE ZONES

The next issue we need to talk about that affects climate on a global scale are the climate zones, and there are four of these. The tropics, subtropics, temperate zones and polar zones. We're going to start at the equator and work our way outwards. And this means that we're going to start our discussion with the tropics.

These run from 0°, which is the equator, to 23.5° latitude. What really defines this is not the latitude, but the spot at which the sun appears to be directly overhead at its highest point in the sky. Naturally, most of us have no idea where that really is, so it's just safe to say that, at least on Earth, it's roughly 23.5°. If your planet is roughly the same size, then it's going to be roughly the same spot. This isn't something we really need to worry about too much other than just having a general sense of where that is. If yours is 23° or 24° on your planet that you're inventing, that's perfectly fine. No one's going to call you out on that and say, "Well, that's not true," because, of course, we're inventing a planet that doesn't exist.

One of the most important aspects of the tropics is that they move the heat away from the equator towards the poles. This is true both in the ocean and in the atmosphere. That said, the tropics are not a climate, they are a climate zone. And what I mean is that if we have colder ocean temperatures, or even warmer ocean temperatures and mountain ranges, these can further modify the climate on the continents. For example, if the water is very cold, then the atmosphere is going to be colder there. And if the mountains are very high, then the air is thinner up there and this is also going to have an affect on the climate.

If this is unclear on exactly how that works, it will become clearer in a few minutes when we talk about the actual climates themselves. Right now, we're talking about climate zones. And what do I really mean about a climate zone? We're talking about a general area, in this case of the tropics, from 0° to 23.5°, and this goes all the way around the Earth, both north and south of the equator. This is a zone. The actual climates that are in that zone are affected by being in that zone, but they may differ from the average, and we're going to talk about that more.

Now, you may have heard the terms "Tropic of Cancer" and "Tropic of Capricorn." These are just the names of the northern and southern tropics, respectively. On an invented world, we're going to want different names for these, and that raises the question of how do you choose a name? Let's say we're talking about the northern tropics and you have a kingdom on one of the continents that is synonymous with the area between the equator and roughly 23.5°. In other words, it's most filling up that area of the tropics. You could name the tropics after that and have that be on your map so that you just call it the "Tropic of Antaria" if the Kingdom of Antaria is filling up that area of the northern tropics.

Now, it's true that in another part of the world they may call it something else, but this is going to depend on how much travel is really happening on your world. And, let's face it, most of us are never going to mention this, so what you call it isn't really that important. However, it can be relatively easy to make up a name like this. And, if you have a sailing story, for example, where a character is travelling into the tropics, it might add a little bit of realism to throw out the name in your narration or in dialogue.

Since the tropics end at roughly 23.5°, they give way to the subtropics, which run from there until about 40°. As you might expect, this area is a little bit cooler. On Earth, most of the world's deserts are in this region. Further from there is the temperate zone, which runs from roughly 40°

latitude to 66° latitude. And this is, arguably, the most important one – at least here on Earth – because the majority of the world's population lives in that zone.

In this zone, coastal areas experience a milder winter and summer than areas that are further inland, which experience a greater range in temperatures. In other words, it's going to be even hotter and colder within the interior of a continent than it is on the coast. And the reason for that is the moisture in the air, and that is caused by the currents in the ocean.

It's also worth noting that if you have a very high-altitude area in this zone, it might essentially act like it's further north in the polar zone. What I mean is that it's essentially going to be a lot colder as if it's further north because of how high it is.

And the last area we need to talk about is the polar zone, which is basically from the pole all the way down to 66° latitude. There isn't really much to say about this that isn't perfectly obvious to all of us.

Now, I recognize that some of that information is kind of dry, but you're in luck because the next two subjects we're going to talk about are prevailing winds and rain shadows, and both of those are actually pretty interesting and have a dramatic impact on where vegetation is and just how we go about laying out a continent or a region of one.

PREVAILING WINDS

Let's talk about prevailing winds. What this means is that the winds are traveling a certain direction based on how far they are from the equator. In other words, how far from the equator those winds are. Fortunately, this is relatively simple. The winds that are closer to the equator in the tropics and subtropics are generally going west. By contrast, the easterly winds are the ones that are in the temperate zone. This is not to say that the winds are due east or due west, which means straight east or west. It means that they are westerly, for example. That means they're going mostly west, but they're kind of northwest.

The reason we care about these winds is that, along with geography like mountains, this will determine where rain falls. And that, in turn, will determine where vegetation and lack of vegetation, like a desert, is. Since the rotation of the Earth is responsible for the direction of these winds, we need to be aware of which direction the Earth is spinning, which is counter-clockwise, and which direction these winds tend to be in different latitudes, as I just mentioned. And the only reason we really need to care about this is that if we decide to change our invented planet so that it's rotating the other way, then all of these winds will also be the opposite direction.

In other words, if the planet is rotating clockwise, then the easterly winds will be those near the equator, and the westerly winds will be those in the temperate zones. I do have a figure, number 17, on the website showing the prevailing winds that will really help get this across.

The biggest reason that we really care about these prevailing winds is that they are going to determine something known as a rain shadow. This is one of the big payoffs for listening to this particular episode of the podcast, because this is really going to have an affect on your continent. What's going to happen is that there is moisture-carrying wind that is approaching a mountain range, and that mountain range will cause the atmosphere and the clouds to rise. And what's going to happen as a result of this is that a lot of that moisture is going to fall on that side of the mountains as rain. One result is going to be lush vegetation on one side of the mountain range. But, as the moisture-carrying winds go over that range, on the other side there is now very little moisture in the atmosphere. And, as a result, there is no rain to fall on the other side, so you're going to end up with a desert. This is called a rain shadow.

A rain shadow can extend as much as a thousand miles away from a mountain range. For example, in the United States, the mountains on the western coast cause a rain shadow, and this is partly responsible for the great plains that fill up the center of the US. Why is that a plain instead of a forest? Well, because there isn't enough moisture to fall out of the sky to cause that kind of vegetation there.

If you want to see this for yourself, go to Google Maps and zoom out on any continent, or even the whole planet, and you can see where there is vegetation on one side of a mountain range and there is usually a barren area of land on the other side. This is definitely something you want to take advantage of when you are laying out your continents and deciding where a forest, mountain and desert are.

THE CLIMATES

The last thing we're going to talk about are the climates themselves and where these are typically found. I'm going to keep this at a high level because it's kind of a lot of information to remember in a podcast episode for you. So, you may already know some of what I'm about to say, but I just want to make sure we're all on the same page. Climate is a long-term weather pattern, rather than the day-to-day changes. There are times in our modern world where someone is talking about climate change, and someone points to the weather today to indicate that there is no climate change occurring, and this is a faulty argument.

Such a person does not understand the difference between climate and weather.

What is that difference? Weather changes from day-to-day. Climate is something that basically stays the same for a long time. But, once it does start to change, that change is gradual and it moves in a certain direction and keeps moving in that direction, which is why we talk about global warming. If global warming will be followed by global cooling, that's not going to be for thousands of years. It's not going to be something that happens tomorrow.

As far as climate goes, there are things that can affect that climate and change what we might expect, given the latitude of the region we're talking about. For example, the terrain, the altitude and nearby bodies of water, and their current, can all impact the climate in a region.

The first kind of climate we want to talk about is tropical, which are those nearest the equator. There are several kinds of tropical climates, including tropical rainforests, tropical monsoon, and tropical wet/dry, which is also known as savannah. For most of us, all we're really going to care about is the tropical rainforest one. So, that's what I'm going to discuss briefly here.

This is usually found within 5 to 10 degrees of the equator but can sometimes extend to as far as 25 degrees away. The thing about this climate is that the seasons do not really happen here, as we were talking about earlier, this close to the equator. Most places are also wet all year round, and a rain shadow is not going to have as big of an affect here because there is just so much water.

Let's move on to the dry climate. Naturally, such an area is known for how little rain it receives. What we really care about here is that there are three types of desert; hot, cold and mild. The hot deserts are sunny all year round, and one of the side affects of this is that they have extremely high temperatures during the day, but at night it also gets really cold. This is almost always found in tropical regions. We're not going to find such a desert in Canada, for example.

By contrast, a cold desert is very hot during the summer, but the winter can be way far below freezing, to the point of it being really dangerous. These are the ones that are usually found in the rain shadow of a mountain. They also occur at really high elevations. These are the ones often found in a temperate zone like in the United States.

Finally, we get to the mild deserts, which are usually mild all year round, and are usually found on the western edge of a continent or at a high altitude. Earlier, we talked about how the western edge of a continent will have colder water, and that is partly responsible for these forming. So, this type of desert is found on the western side of continents. That also means near the coast.

What does all this mean for us? Well, we should have some idea of what kind of desert forms where, if we are intending to have our characters traveling through one of them so that we can characterize it appropriately and distinguish one from another so that they're not all the same.

Next, we get to the temperate climates. And, once again, there are a half-dozen varieties of these that I'm not going to cover in detail. This is where most of the Earth's population lives, and that's partly because that's where most of the land is. These climates have all four seasons. I could go into detail about all of these, but I have a feeling they would put you to sleep. If you are really interested in this, I would suggest looking at the website, Artofworldbuilding.com, and I do have a chart listing all of these out and making it relatively easy for you to understand them. It is Figure 19, the climate chart.

The next climate we should mention is humid continental. And what this means is these are the ones found in the interior of a continent, away from the coast. Once again, there are a half-dozen varieties of this. These are also found on the eastern side of continents because of the warm, humid air there. Forests grow really well in this climate, including evergreens and conifers. Rain tends to fall equally in all seasons. These differences and more are also summed up in the chart that I referenced earlier.

The only climate left is the polar one, but you basically know what this one is. It's very cold.

CONCLUSION

So, to conclude our discussion about climate, I think the big take-aways for you are to just understand the equator's role and the ocean's role, and where there tends to be warmer and colder water. You know, as far as which side of the continent. And then understanding the zones, the prevailing winds and the rain shadows are the big ones.

As far as the specific climates, I would use that chart that I have on the website and go through that anytime you are getting ready to set a story in a given city because you can decide what the weather is basically going to be like from year to year, and whether it's going to be rainy or dry or really humid. And there are areas of different countries that are known for the weather.

You know, in the United States, the southeastern area is known for being really humid and hot. By contrast, in the southwestern area, it's known for being really hot, but dry. So, this is the kind of difference that you might want to talk about when your characters are in a story, because, otherwise, you might just be tempted to make every place look like it's exactly the same. And we can create a better sense of realism by doing something with these climates.

HOW TO CREATE
A CONTINENT

Hello and welcome to *The Art of World Building Podcast*, episode number twelve. Today's topic is how to create a continent, including hemisphere considerations, understanding plate tectonics, and when to use what term for bodies of water, like oceans, seas, bays, and more. This material and more is discussed in chapter 3 of *Creating Places*, volume 2 in *The Art of World Building* book series

HOW MANY CONTINENTS TO BUILD

While we are talking about creating a continent today, we're looking at the big picture. And that means we're not talking about mountain ranges and forests, prairies, grasslands and other details like cities. We will be talking about all of those things, but those will be covered by different episodes that dive more deeply into those subjects. Regardless of how many continents we are creating, the same advice and procedures can apply to doing all of them. For any continent that we create, we don't have to create every last detail of it, especially if we're not going to use it.

It helps to have an idea of what you're going to use it for. Something like a a trilogy or a long novel where the characters are going from one place to another and collecting quest tokens, as they're called, is going to need more places developed. On the other hand, if you're writing a short story, you certainly don't need to go that far. However, that said, even if you're just focused on a local region, it will help to know where the equator is in relation to your story, and how far away the mountain ranges are and what the weather patterns are like. So, it does help to have that broader image in your head, but this can be general for most of the continent and go into detail just on the area that you're going to actually use.

One reason we want to have at least a general sense of other areas on the continent is that we may be able to refer to them. Let's say that we have a country called Outlandia and we can just say, from Outlandia, they have great wines. And that might be the only thing that we have invented for that place. This might be all that we ever do with that, but then, maybe later, we decide to actually use Outlandia. And, at that point, we start fleshing it out more.

One reason I mention this is that it can become overwhelming to think about creating the details of an entire continent. So, in the beginning, we just want to focus on some basics, and that's what we start with. This same idea can apply whether we're talking about different areas of one continent or multiple continents. If the idea of creating one continent feels overwhelming, then that gets exponentially worse if we're talking about multiple continents. But sometimes all we need to do is name them and decide which direction they are in from the one that we're currently working on. We may never use them, we may never mention them, but if we decide to use them later, then at least they exist and we already know where they are in relation to our first continent.

MIGRATION AND SKIN COLOR

Another reason to go ahead and create these other areas of a continent or other continents is that travelers from faraway lands may reach our shores eventually and become integrated into the local world that we're creating — the local area that we are intending to use. Using Earth as an example, and just the United States, the native population had darker skin than white people from Europe. Black people from Africa, of course, had even darker skin. Unless you are planning to populate your story with people who are exclusively one race, which means they are from one geographic area, then you may want to have an idea where other races could have come from. And by races, I don't mean dwarves and elves, but races of humans.

You've probably heard of the recent controversy about the whitewashing of Hollywood and how films sometimes show only white actors, even when the location is ancient Africa, and that is something that bothers people. Now, whether you agree with that or not, it is still true that the skin color of people in one region is going to be determined by their location comparative to where the equator is. Since the equator is hotter, then people there tend to wear less clothing. And, as a result, they are exposed to much more sun. And, over the millennia, their skin is more likely to darken. By contrast, someone who is living closer to the poles is usually covered up when they're outside, and this does not happen.

This is a very general concept, but what you want to do is have at least some idea where the white people came from and where the black people came from, just using those two as an example. If they're from the same continent, then you still need to know where the equator lies on the continent that you are creating, and then you need to understand how far away each region that you are drawing is from that equator. If the continent that you're creating is relatively small, then you're probably going to have a skin tone that is pretty similar throughout.

That means if there are people of a different skin color there, then they must have come from another continent. And it's probably going to help you to know how far away that is, which will determine how likely it is that people from there end up here. If we don't want to invent that other continent in detail, then all we have to do is choose an area on that continent, give it a name and then we are good to go for now. And if we ever decide to return to that and develop it in more detail, well, we've already got it.

In fantasy, travel is typically far less likely when we're talking about great distances than in a sci-fi setting. So, in sci-fi, we're probably going to have much more integration. But of course, in sci-fi, the problem may be exponentially worse because, in that case, you might be talking about multiple planets and even multiple solar systems. But, once again, we don't have to create all of those in great detail. Just create what you're actually going to use.

GETTING STARTED

There's a fairly simple process you can do to get started with creating a continent. The first step would be to roughly draw one on a sheet of paper, and not worry about how great it looks because no one's ever going to see this except for you. Then you should decide where that landmass lies in relation to the equator, and where it is in relation to any other continent. And that can be as simple as drawing an arrow pointing to the right side of the page and writing "Outlandia" and indicating it is in that direction.

Then, of course, you're going to want to give that continent a name. Now, you might just give it a working name for now because that might not be the best thing. For example, I made up Outlandia a couple minutes ago, and I would never actually use that because, personally, I don't think it sounds very smart. But it just gives me a working title to use for now and I can replace it later.

Once we have a continent drawn in rough form, we can start carving it up into sovereign powers. Now, that said, I will recommend that you draw more features on that continent, such as mountain ranges and forests, because in my experience, when those are there I can often use those to figure out what might be where as far as countries go. If you'd like a really detailed explanation of what I mean, I would suggest picking up a copy of *Creating Places*, and I think it's Chapter 1. It talks about case studies.

This is a detailed breakdown of exactly what I was thinking when I created certain areas of one of my continents and how I used land features like forests, mountains, even the sea to determine where those countries broke down in between one and another, or what the boundary was. And then the reason they are that way, and even how I decided, based on land features, what the government type was and whether it was an aggressive or peaceful country, whether they have freedoms or slavery. And all of that is discussed in detail in that one chapter. And that's one of the few chapters — and, so far, the only chapter — that I'm not covering at all during this podcast because it's a little too map specific. You need to be looking at the maps that I have in that chapter in order to follow along.

At least one of those case studies is published on artofworldbuilding.com. If you go to the menu for Book Two, there's a link that says "read free." You can get to the table of contents on there and you can go to that section and just read some of what I'm talking about.

Now, once we've got our sovereign powers decided, we are once again going to need some names for these. And we can follow the same process of just giving them some basic names that we can improve later. In my experience, names are sometimes hard to come up with. And we're going to discuss this in another podcast episode as part of Volume 3, *Cultures and Beyond*, but there are techniques we can use to come up with names. And one of the things that happens is that anytime we are inventing names, not every name is going to be great the first time we try to come up with one. So, in my experience, I have repeatedly replaced names that I just didn't like, or it was okay, but in time I thought, "Okay. I'm finally going to fix that."

So, that brings up a basic problem with world building, or just a situation with world building, where generally we are often improving on what we've created. That comes up a little bit less with short stories because we're probably going to invent the world, and the story outline and then write the story and not revisit that.

That last thing we might want to do at a high level when creating these sovereign powers is just to decide what kind of sovereign power they are. Our choices are things like authoritative states, democracies, federations and monarchies. We're going to cover a lot more of that when we get to creating a sovereign power. So, in the beginning, all we really need to do is have a basic understanding of whether this is a benevolent or nefarious society. Is this somewhere where people have freedom and it's relatively peaceful, or is it really horrible to live there? We can decide later what sort of government is responsible for that quality of life.

We can also decide that certain areas of the continent have a reputation for one thing or another. Think about the Earth and what intrigues us about a place. Some countries are known for their benevolence while others are known for being a source of tension. That would include the Middle East. Other areas are known for their dictatorships and the brutal quality of life. An area might also be known for its hot and humid weather or its hot and dry weather. There's at least one area on Earth that is synonymous with brutally frigid cold.

More examples include a slave trade, huge forests, impenetrable mountains, vast deserts and exotic animals. Mind you that exotic animals are only going to seem exotic to people who are from another place. To the locals, they're going to seem normal. But this is one of the reasons to create this sort of reputation for certain areas and then reference them in the area where you set your story.

WHICH HEMISPHERE?

The next subject we're going to talk about is a brief one, and that is the affect of the hemisphere where your continent is located. One reason I'm not going to spend too much time on this is that the previous two episodes talked about this in more detail. We can draw something like a mountain range without having decided where our continent lies in relation to the equator, but we shouldn't draw things like deserts, grasslands or forests without having made this decision.

The reason is that all of those are going to be affected by where the continent lies in relation to the equator. One reason for this is the prevailing winds and the latitude. And then, of course, there's the influence of those mountain ranges. The previous episodes talk about the subject of rain shadows, which basically means that the prevailing winds are moving in a given direction, and when they hit a mountain range, those winds go up and all of the water — well, not all of it, but most of the water in the clouds falls on one side of the mountain range, and then, on the other side, there's no water left to fall. As a result, there is usually a desert there, and this is known as a rain shadow.

How do we know which direction the prevailing winds are blowing and which side of the mountain range is going to have forest and which will have desert? That's easy. It's going to be based on the latitude, which means the distance from the equator, which is why we need to know this. It changes depending on how far from the equator you are. I don't want to reexplain all of this, so if you haven't listened to Episode 11.1 or 11.2, go ahead and check those out after this one.

One last issue to talk about is that if you are living in a given continent, you are used to thinking that it's colder in one direction and warmer in another, but this is going to be reversed if you are in the other hemisphere. This is a big deal when you're creating a continent because you don't want to be creating a cold region to the north if you later decide that this continent is in the Southern Hemisphere. Because the colder region is actually going to be to the south and the northern area is going to be warm.

Another issue is that the seasons are reversed. When it is winter in the northern hemisphere, it is, of course, summer in the southern hemisphere. The entire planet is not experiencing winter or summer at the same time.

PLATE TECTONICS AND MOUNTAINS/VOLCANOES

If you're like me, you learned about plate tectonics either in junior or high school, but you've probably forgotten some of the details. So, we're going to discuss some of the basics you need to know when inventing a continent.

The biggest reason that this matters is that plate tectonics are going to determine where your mountain ranges are. This is not to suggest that we actually have to figure out where the plate outlines are when we are inventing a continent, but just to get a general understanding of what's going to happen and what is not going to happen.

For example, I once drew a continent that had a circular mountain range. This is basically impossible. The only explanation for that is that those mountains were part of a range and they were once filled on, but then some sort of titanic explosion happened and carved out the center. I made that decision when I was a teenager when I couldn't have cared less about being correct. But that's the kind of mistake we would likely want to avoid. If you're wondering how I solved that problem later, when I wised up — well, I just told you. I decided that a huge explosion had created this situation. With some ingenuity, there is often a way out of our mistakes, but it is better to avoid those mistakes in the first place.

In theory, that's one of the reasons you're listening to this podcast. So, let's get started.

A planet like the Earth is composed of an outermost shell of slowly moving plates, and those plates either move towards each other, which is called convergence, or they move away from each other, which is called divergence, or they transform. We'll talk more about that last one in a minute. The converging or diverging ones are what give us mountain ranges and volcanos. Most of the volcanos occur where two plate boundaries intersect, but some of the volcanos can exist in the middle of a plate due to a flaw in the plate. And what that means is that the crust of the earth could be unusually thin right there. And, as a result, the magma below the surface is able to burst through and create a volcano.

So, one thing that this means is that we could have a volcano anywhere on our map and no one can tell us, "No, that's not possible." I can almost hear some of you breathing a sigh of relief the same way that I did.

Since I live in the United States, I'm more familiar with what's going on on either coast and I'm going to use this country as an example of something. The west coast, with California, is known for earthquakes, but the eastern coast is not. And there is a reason for this. Every continent, obviously, has an area that is above water. But, just off shore, there is an area of the continental shelf that is underwater. This is an area of relatively shallow water compared to the deeper sea that is farther away. On the west coast, the continental shelf ends relatively near the end of the actual continent, but on the east coast the continental shelf is relatively farther away.

This is something that we can decide almost arbitrarily when we are inventing our own continents. After all, no one from this invented planet we are making up is going to come to Earth and tell us that we're wrong.

One thing that this means is that deep ocean is just off shore on the west coast, but on the east coast it is farther away. And one of the things that this implies is that if we are creating the sort of world that has sea monsters, they are more likely to be close to the western side of the United States, in this example, than the eastern side of the

United States, if we are deciding that those sea monsters are truly enormous and prefer having deep water to live in.

The more important aspect of this is that the plate boundary is near the west coast of the United States, and that means that this causes dramatic activity at the boundary between the two plates. What kind of dramatic activity? Mountain ranges, volcanos and earthquakes. So, something to keep in mind is that if there is deep water just off shore, that also would imply that there are probably mountains and volcanos on the continent right there.

One of the challenges of world building is that we sometimes don't really have a reason for making one choice or another, and, therefore, we get stuck by indecision. This is one way to get past that. If we would like sea monsters that prefer deep water to be near the eastern side of the continent, then we are probably going to have tall mountain ranges and volcanos there. If we don't have a sea monster idea or story in mind, then we can still just make this decision somewhat arbitrarily but understand what we are implying. A shipwreck on the eastern coast of the United States is likely to be in relatively shallow water compared to one off the western coast of the United States, unless that shipwreck is relatively close to the continent.

Convergent Boundaries

Let's talk about convergent boundaries. What this means is that two plates are moving together and one of them is destroying the edge of the other. The results of this can be varied. One result is called subduction, and this means that one plate is forced under the other. This often happens when the two plates are for an ocean and a continent. This is known as an ocean-to-continent boundary. When this happens, the ocean plate is the one that goes under the continent, and this causes a mountain range that is on that side of the continent, such as the western side of the US.

One thing this means is that that mountain range will be parallel to the coast. So, if the coast is running north to south, the mountain range is, too. And the volcanos that are here are usually very explosive. In fact, they are the most explosive volcanos on earth. Of course, one of the things this means is that the residents on such a coast should be aware of volcanos. Depending on how well they keep written records, they may be well aware of when the last eruption was. They might also have myths about this and cultural milestones, such as the last time that eruption took place, because that might have destroyed the city or something else that's very important to everyone.

Another scenario is that we could have two ocean plates where one is being forced under the other. What this causes is a chain of volcanos, just like those in Hawaii.

Then there is the continent-to-continent boundary. And when this happens, the plates converge, fold and lift, forming very tall mountain ranges with no volcanos. These are the tallest mountain ranges on the world, and they are located in the interior of the continents. When drawing a map or deciding on where things are, this is something we should consider.

DIVERGENT BOUNDARIES

Earlier, I mentioned another kind of boundary, and that is the divergent boundary, when two plates are moving away from each other. If this happens underwater, this can also from volcanic islands. If this happens on land instead, what happens is that a low area of land can form and then possibly fill with ocean water to create a sea, such as with the Mediterranean Sea.

You may have heard this idea that the Earth once had a super continent, which I think was called Pangea. The reason this broke apart was divergent plates. The plates moved away from each other. Evidence of this can be seen just by looking at a map, because the left side, or the western side, of Africa looks like it fits into the right side, or eastern side, of South America like they're some sort of jigsaw puzzle. We may want to consider this when drawing two continents, because we could draw the right side of one to be a mirror image of the left side of another one.

Sometimes, as world builders, we are looking for a reason to make a decision, and this can be one way to achieve that decision. Not only can we decide what one side of a continent looks like, but we can decide on what another side of a different continent looks like. However, don't go overboard. Don't make every single edge of every continent look like it fits into some sort of jigsaw puzzle.

Transform Boundaries

The last type of boundary is called a transform boundary, and this means that two plates are grinding past each other without either of them getting destroyed. This causes really strong earthquakes, but, aside from this, there's no evidence, like mountains or volcanos, that they actually exist unless we are a scientist studying this sort of thing. What this means for us as world builders is that we can basically ignore this type of boundary. It's not going to affect what we indicate exists on a map. On the other hand, we could decide that there are strong earthquakes somewhere that is far from a mountain range, and that this is the reason for it.

One way to tell that such a boundary exists is if a road that used to connect has a break in that road that is 20, 30, or more feet apart from each other. We could have our characters see that a road they are following suddenly ends, but that it is continuing but it's 30 feet away. In doing so, we would be implying that this area is prone to extremely strong earthquakes.

HOW TO NAME WATER BODIES

There's one more major subject that we should discuss when we are creating a continent, and that is the bodies of water that are surrounding that continent. Here on Earth, we talk about there being five different oceans, and those are the Pacific, Atlantic, Indian, Arctic and Southern oceans, but the reality is that these are all one, continuous body of water that is a kind of world ocean. Why did we divide them up? Because it makes it easier to refer to one area of that ocean versus another. Also bear in mind that sometimes we talk about there being Northern Pacific and a Southern Pacific Ocean, for example. This is done for the same reason. These are really the same body of water.

One of the things that we're talking about right now is why different bodies of water are named different things. For example, you may have wondered what the difference between an ocean and a sea is. The quick answer to that is that there is actually no difference. This is one reason why we can all be confused about that. We're assuming that there is a difference, otherwise why would people have two different words? But I guess people just like to use different words for the same thing. It's called a synonym.

That said, the word "sea" is typically used to refer to a smaller area than an ocean, and it is often an area that is surrounded by land on several sides. What that means is that it's going to be near a continent, of course. There is, of course, something called a lake, and one of the differences between a lake and a sea is that a lake is completely surrounded by land, whereas a sea is only partially surrounded by it. That said, sometimes a very large lake is called a sea, and there could be several reasons for this. One of those might be that technology is not great and, therefore, the people who are living on one shore of that lake feel like the lake extends indefinitely, and it might extend so far out of reach that they think it's a sea when it isn't.

There's another reason to call a lake a sea, and that is simply because the name might sound better. The Sea of Sadness sounds more interesting than the Lake of Sadness. Another explanation is that the word "sea" can often have a connotation that the land on the far side of that sea is somehow untamed and wild. And, therefore, it is dangerous. You may have noticed that we are basically using the wrong word, sea, to refer to a lake, but that we can sometimes get away with this and justify it, although we don't necessarily have to explain to our audience why we have chosen that name.

One point here is if real people on Earth are using the wrong word for something, then there's certainly no reason we can't use it, too. One problem to be aware of though is that there will be people who think they know everything. They're a know-it-all, and they could come along and say, "Well, you don't know what you're talking about." But we do have some flexibility here.

When we are creating our continent, there are other words we can use to refer to different areas of the edge of that continent where it meets the water. I'm going to quickly run through some of those. Like a sea, a bay is a body of water that is surrounded on several sides by land and it can be part of an ocean or a lake. A gulf is a very large bay. A cove is a smaller bay and is usually circular, with a narrow passage that leads into it or out of it. A fjord is a narrow bay with a steep terrain on either side of it, or, usually, both sides of it. An inlet is a narrow, but long, indentation of shoreline and which often connects a bay to another body of water. There could be a group of these, and those are often called a sound. A sound is large enough to draw on a continent-sized map, and they can be big, if not bigger, than a bay. Finally, if there are two large bodies of water that are separated by a narrow area of water, that smaller area is called a strait, channel, pass or passage.

If you're having trouble remembering all of that, then you could pick up a copy of *Creating Places*, and Chapter 3 has all of this listed out for you.

HOW TO CREATE LAND FEATURES

Hello and welcome to *The Art of World Building Podcast*, episode number thirteen, part one. Today's topic is how to create land features, including mountains, volcanoes, rivers, lakes, and various kinds of forests, from woodlands to savannahs, jungles, and run-of-the-mill forests. This material and more is discussed in chapter 4 of *Creating Places*, volume two in *The Art of World Building* book series.

CREATING MOUNTAINS

Mountains are the first land feature we're going to talk about because they have a big effect on where forests, deserts, and bodies of water, like rivers and lakes, will form. In the previous episode, number 12, we talked about plate tectonics and how this determines what kind of mountain ranges are in what location. I don't want to explain that over again, so if you missed that episode, I suggest checking that out. I would also suggest checking out the previous episode, number 11, where I talked about prevailing winds and rain shadows.

I'll briefly mention the reason we care about this, and basically what is going on is that wind is moving in a certain direction based on how far from the equator that landmass is and where the wind is passing over it. What happens is that the prevailing winds hit one side of the mountains and most of the water in those clouds falls on that side, causing a forest there and, on the other side, there is no more rain to fall. And, as a result, there's usually a desert there. This is one of the reasons we care about putting mountains on our map first. Or, even if we're not doing a map, this is something we should decide on early.

But let's talk about the mountains themselves, not the affect that they have on vegetation. We all think we know what a mountain is, but it might surprise you to know that there is actually no definition that has been agreed upon. For something to be considered a mountain, it just has to be something that stands out from the surrounding countryside. So, if you have a very flat land and there is a so-called mountain that is 2,000 feet tall, then it's going to look like a mountain. Calling it one might seem ridiculous to someone who is used to living somewhere where the mountains are 14,000 feet tall, but it's still okay to call it that. For this reason, when we are doing world building and we are deciding that there's a range of mountains, or even just a solitary peak, we should always make a note in our files just how big this thing is.

On Earth, roughly a quarter of the surface is covered in mountains. So, when you are laying out your continent, you should have this understanding that these are not exactly rare. Depending on the size of the continent that we're inventing, there could be multiple mountain ranges. Sometimes mountain ranges are parallel to each other.

Using the US as an example, all of them run north to south. The Cascade Mountains on the western coast do this, and so do the Rocky Mountains that are further inland. And the same is true on the eastern side of the US.

One thing to keep in mind is that to the average person like ourselves, when we look at a map showing the topography, we might think that the Cascade Mountains on the western side of the United States is one very long mountain range going all the way from Canada down through the United States into Mexico. But the reality is that these are actually separate mountain ranges that are sort of stacked on top of each other north to south.

If we choose to do such a thing, we may want to leave a small gap in between those mountain ranges and indicate that this is a travel route (or a pass, as we sometimes call them) or we might want to just decide to use one name for the entire range. And, in fact, this sort of thing does happen in the real world. We do that with the east coast mountains. For example, the Blue Ridge Mountains and the Shenandoah Mountains are actually part of the larger Appalachian Mountain Range. If we don't want to invent three different names like that, then we don't have to.

Many of us have probably heard of Olympus Mons on Mars. This is the largest mountain in the entire solar system. On Earth, Mount Everest is roughly 29,000 feet, but Olympus Mons is 69,000 feet. This seems like it would be truly amazing, but the reality is that the mountain is so large – it's basically the size of France – that if you were standing on that mountain, you wouldn't even realize you were on a mountain because it's so broad and flat. The reason this mountain is so tall is that there are no tectonic plates on Mars. And we discussed that in a previous episode. Basically, all of the continents we have here on Earth are on top of a tectonic plate which is sort of floating on the surface of the Earth. They're all basically moving.

When they move towards each other or they pull apart, this causes volcanoes and mountain ranges to form.

There's also something called a hot spot, and this is actually what's causing Olympus Mons. Basically, the surface of Mars is not moving and there is a hot spot there. Therefore, the magma is just perpetually coming up. This doesn't happen on Earth to the same degree because the surface of the Earth is moving. And, therefore, the hot spot keeps changing as well and that gives us something like the volcanic islands of Hawaii.

One point I'm getting at here is that a truly enormous mountain is only going to happen on a world where there are no tectonic plates, and that's going to cause all sorts of other changes to our world that we might want to be aware of. For example, all of the other kinds of mountain ranges are probably not going to exist. As a result, those mountain ranges that don't exist are not going to have an affect on prevailing winds, and there's not going to be this whole thing of rain shadows and forests on one side, and then deserts on the other.

Of course, anything is technically possible, and scientists often say something like that, and then, years later, they discover a world that has something that they thought was impossible. So, maybe I'm wrong, but you get the idea. If you're going to do something like one truly enormous mountain, you're implying that there are no tectonic plates and that there would be other side effects. However, the average person reading your book is going to have no idea about any of that.

This means we could get away with a truly enormous mountain, but if you stop and think about it, a solitary mountain is the most impressive looking thing. One example that you can Google to get some images of this is Mount Shasta in Northern California. It's the only mountain right there and it stands out very dramatically from the surrounding because of that. And it's only 14,000 feet tall, compared to Mount Everest at 29,000 feet. And then, of course, there is Olympus Mons at over 69,000 feet.

When I see pictures of Mount Everest, it doesn't look nearly as majestic to me as Mount Shasta, even though it's twice as tall, because there are all sorts of other mountains that are almost as tall surrounding Mount Everest. But, on the other hand, Mount Shasta is kind of standing there mostly by itself. In other words, context is everything.

VOLCANOES

In thinking about volcanoes, one of the things that we need to concern ourselves with is its status. Some volcanoes are said to be extinct, and what that really means is that in written history it has never erupted. Now, if we have a species like elves that are 1,000 years old, and they have a civilization going very far back, then your world might have no volcanoes that are considered to be extinct. Or we could change our definition from extinct meaning "that no written record of it erupting exists" to "no living memory of it erupting exists either." Or we could decide that extinct just means it's 5,000 years since it erupted. In Earth terms, that's long enough ago to be before written history. Actually, that may not be true, but you get the idea.

An extinct volcano has not erupted in thousands of years. So, what do we call one that has erupted in the last few thousand years or during written history? Well, those are called dormant if they are not currently active. And, of course, an active volcano is erupting right now. You're not going to fail to notice this. Neither are your characters. As storytellers, we only need an active volcano when that's actually going to impact the story that we're telling.

Extinct volcanoes may not have much use for us because it's no fun deciding that something is never going to erupt again and, in fact, we're right about that. It can be more fun to decide that people think it's extinct and that it's not going to erupt again, but it's actually dormant and then, suddenly, it erupts. But, of course, just as with the active volcanoes, once it's erupting, that's going to be impacting our story. So, we only need to be concerned about that if it's going to be something we want to happen.

In other words, should we bother putting a volcano there if it's extinct, or should we always decide that those are dormant? In other words, we're not going to use it until, suddenly, we do need it. Bear in mind that even with a supposedly extinct volcano, it's possible for us to have geological cataclysms of such a huge nature that a once extinct volcano becomes one that's erupting.

Also bear in mind that, just like you were a few minutes ago, probably, your characters don't really know the difference between dormant and extinct. All they're really going to be thinking is whether or not that's going to erupt anytime soon, and that's going to be based on how recently it last erupted, which means it's dormant. If everyone says, "Well, we don't remember it ever erupting," well then, of course, it's extinct. But no one's probably going to make those distinctions. The exception would be a scientist.

CHARACTERIZING MOUNTAINS

When we're creating mountains, we should also try to characterize these just as we do with volcanoes. We could reasonably say that mountain ranges are roughly in the 3,000 to 4,000 foot range, which is around 900 meters, or they tower over 10,000 feet or over 3,000 meters. Making a distinction here is one way to keep all of your mountain ranges from being the same. If the continent you're inventing is going to have two mountain ranges, make one of them small and the other one big. How do you decide? Well, from the previous episode on plate tectonics, you might remember that the tallest mountain ranges tend to be those on the interior of the continent. They also don't have volcanoes.

On the other hand, those mountain ranges along the coasts do have volcanoes and tend to be shorter. This isn't necessarily the case, however, as the mountains on the eastern side of the US are in the roughly 3,000 to 4,000 foot range, whereas the tallest mountains on the western coast are in that 14,000 range. This might sound contradictory, but basically, that's the way nature works. Nothing is really a law set in stone, and the great thing about this is that this gives us flexibility to decide what we want to do. We can be informed by science instead of restricted by it.

The lower mountains are less likely to cause the rain shadow that we've talked about in a couple episodes here. On the other hand, taller mountains will definitely cause one. This is why we see rain shadows on the western side of the US, but we do not see them on the eastern side.

Tall mountains are harder to get over, not only for those on land, but even for birds. It may surprise you to know that in the Himalayas, there are species of birds that try to traverse those mountains and they have a lot of difficulty flying that high to do so. If you have dragons in your world, or enormous birds like eagles that you see in *The Lord of the Rings*, this is also going to affect them. And it might affect them even more than the smaller birds.

So, if you're trying to decide how tall the mountains should be for your story, then this is one way to make a decision. If you would like the dragons to have to also go around, then there you go. You could just make these mountains very tall. That said, we do like the idea that dragons are all-powerful, but it's really a good idea in any sort of storytelling to give even something supposedly that powerful some sort of weakness. This is a very realistic and believable one for dragons.

The higher the mountains, the less likely they are traversed, which means that there may be fewer trade routes or settlements there. This, in turn, makes it a good place for a hideout for something like a wizard. In science fiction, this is less true because, of course, we usually have spacecraft and something like that is not really an issue.

RIVERS

Let's talk a little bit about rivers. They obviously flow downhill because that's the way gravity works. And, usually, they end up either in a lake or an ocean. But, sometimes, they actually dry up first. They can also fall into something like a sinkhole in the ground and become an underground river. This is something we can leverage if we have a humanoid species, for example, who lives in water. The result could be that the species is found in places where people might not be expecting them. There could be an underground river nearby.

As for what determines where a river flows, it's generally going to go through the softest material. In other words, it's going to erode dirt before it's going to erode rock. We may also want to keep in mind something called a flood plain. This is where the water goes when the river overflows its banks, and a flood plain can be many miles wide and have settlements in it. So, this is where we want to focus on this. Decide if you have any settlements that are built in a flood plain near a major wide river. If so, they have likely been flooded repeatedly, and this is something that you can add to their history file and it's part of their life there that they expect this. Maybe they've even built their houses on stilts because of it.

The age of a river is something else to consider. If a river is steep and fast, it also tends to be relatively straight. So, if you draw a straight river on your map, you are implying that it's a young river that is steep and fast. It might also be deep instead of broad because the water is going through there so quickly that it's carving a deeper channel.

Then there are mature rivers which are less steep and they flow more slowly. And this is going to mean that they have a wider channel and more tributaries.

And then there are the old rivers. These are slow and they don't erode much anymore. And they usually have a flood plain.

If we are drawing a map, we should be aware that there are many more waterways than the ones that we're going to draw, especially if we're doing a continent-sized map. If we were to draw every little river or stream, the entire thing would be covered in rivers. What this means is that we usually want to make a decision on what the major rivers are, and only depict those. Don't get carried away with putting every other little river onto the map.

When it comes to lakes, sometimes we have a hard time deciding where a lake should be when we're drawing a map. Well, one thing to consider is that they tend to be at higher elevations. This means that we might want to draw it closer to the mountain range than the sea, for example. However, we can really get away with doing almost anything we want here and not explain it. All that really matters is that there is an area of depressed land, and that is where the water has begun to collect.

On Earth, most lakes are freshwater, but not all of them are. So, it is possible to have a saltwater lake. It's also possible to have a lake that does not have a river flowing out the other side. Most of them do because this is how the river maintains its water level. The lakes that don't have a river causing this outflow of water are going to lose their water through evaporation. This is, again, something we don't need to explain to anyone, but there is a tendency to always want to have a river coming out of a lake on one side and going in on the other. And we don't necessarily have to do that. Generally, you will want to do it, however.

There are some other interesting details on lakes and rivers that are found in *Creating Places*, but I'm not going to cover them here.

TYPES OF FORESTS

Arguably, most of us are not that familiar with the different types of forests. And, as a result, we tend to make all of them mostly be the same in our work. So, what we're going to focus on here is discussing some of the differences of the main types. In Episode 8, I talked about the different types of trees. So, we're not going to cover that. We're just going to focus on the different types of forests. That said, it does help to know the basic types of trees. There are evergreens, which are literally green all year. Then there are coniferous ones, which have needle-like leaves such as pine trees. And then there are the deciduous ones, which have seasonal loss of flowers, leaves and fruit ripening.

As it turns out, all trees are actually losing their leaves throughout the year. The issue with deciduous trees is that they do so all at once in a dry season or a winter season, and that's the one that we associate with losing leaves. But, as someone who has a pine tree in his back yard, I can tell you that I spend all year sweeping off my deck because the pine needles just keep falling off. This is on my mind because I literally did this about three hours ago.

REGULAR FORESTS

To talk about the other types of forests, we need to establish a baseline that we will just call the run-of-the-mill forest. This is the one that we will distinguish the other types from. So, what's a forest? Well, that means it has a tree canopy covering roughly 60 to 100 percent of the land under it. In other words, this has one of the thickest tree canopies and, as a result, the most shade is found under it. If we have decided to invent a plant that needs full sun to grow, then it's probably not going to be found in this forest unless it's along the edge of a clearing, for example. There may not be enough sunlight, but it depends on how thick that canopy is. If we've decided that it's covering 100 percent of the land, then yes, that's true. On the other hand, if it's only covering 60 percent of the land, well then, there's probably enough sunlight in certain areas for that to grow.

This is the kind of detail that can add some realism to our story if we've decided the characters are hunting for that plant, but they have to go, say, further into the forest to get to an area that is less full of canopy, and it has more sunlight. But, by doing so, they're going to run into some nasty thing that they're going to have to fight. Why would they want that plant? Well, because it has some sort of property, like magical or poison, that we need for our story. This amount of tree canopy also means that there will be some underbrush, but it's not going to be impenetrable.

WOODLANDS

The next thing we want to talk about is the woodland. Now, we might not call it that on our map. We might just still write the word "forest" or "woods," but we should note in our files that this is a woodland once we understand what that is and why we would want to create one.

The trees in a woodland are spaced further out, and that means that the canopy is less and, therefore, it's relatively sunny. Rather than calling a forest a light forest, we should call it a woodland because that's what it is. There tends to be less underbrush and, therefore, it's relatively easy to ride horses or other animals through a woodland than a forest, or a jungle, certainly. Keep this in mind when deciding what type of forest is in your story. If you want the characters to be able to ride through there relatively quickly, then you say it's a woodland. If you want it to be harder to get through, then maybe it's a forest with more underbrush. Of course, in both cases, they may have trails going through there that bypass this problem, but you get the idea. If they leave the trail, then they have a different degree of difficulty going through the land anyway.

This would also be true for anything living in there that might want to attack our characters. Is the road needed or can they go off that road without suffering any major consequences to their travel time? As you might imagine, if you're a creature who would like to attack travelers, it's easier to do so in a forest than a woodland, partly because there's less to hide behind, but, in a forest, the characters you want to attack might be more restricted to the road and, therefore, it's easier to know where they're going to be. If we've invented a species that is known for attacking travelers in forests, they probably aren't known for doing that in a woodland. So, if you've created two forests – well, one's a forest and one's a woodland, that species might be in one, but not in the other so much.

SAVANNA

And then there's a savanna, which has almost no tree canopy at all, despite the trees. One result is that there could be grass, and it could be rather tall grass that could be hiding things like a lion, for example. If you're wondering where a savanna would be located, well, it's usually between a forest and a grassland. In other words, the thick trees have given away to sparser trees of the savanna, and those eventually give way to the grassland. We shouldn't be afraid to create a savanna because a fifth of the worlds land surface is actually comprised of savannas.

JUNGLES

The last type I want to talk about is the jungle. And this is a term that can be poorly understood for a number of reasons. Sometimes the word "jungle" is confused for the word "rainforest," but to understand that explanation, you'd first need to understand what a jungle is.

It's basically a very dense forest with enough underbrush for it to be difficult, if not impossible, to get through unless you cut your way through. By contrast, a rainforest has very little underbrush because the tree canopy prevents light from reaching the ground, which means that it isn't going to grow. So, the impassable jungle often borders a rainforest because there is enough light at the edge to allow that thick underbrush to grow. You would have to cut your way through it in order to reach the deeper area where it's going to be a rainforest, and there is not going to be all that underbrush.

So, why does a jungle and a rainforest get confused for each other? Well, it's because European explorers were initially traveling through tropical rainforests by river, and what happened is that because the river is opening up the forest there, there is enough sunlight to cause a jungle. It's growing on the edge. So, basically, they thought, wrongly, that the jungle continued miles in each direction away from the river when the reality is if they had just cut their way through a little bit more, they would have seen that it's just a rainforest and that the jungle is only by the river.

We can use this in our stories by having our characters basically make the same mistake. So, we could have a settlement that's in a rainforest and that's only reachable by boat on a river, and people assume that you have to get through this incredibly hard jungle underbrush to get there. And, therefore, people don't even try without even realizing that maybe they only have to cut their way through, I don't know, maybe 1,000 yards of jungle before they suddenly have much easier travel time through the rainforest for the rest of the trip.

HOW TO CREATE LAND FEATURES

Hello and welcome to *The Art of World Building Podcast*, episode number thirteen, part two. Today's topic concludes our discussion about how to create land features. This includes grasslands, deserts, and various kinds of wetlands like bogs, mires, and fens. This material and more is discussed in chapter 4 of *Creating Places*, volume 2 in *The Art of World Building* book series.

GRASSLANDS AND PRAIRIES

Let's briefly talk about grasslands, which can also be called prairies. As the word "grasslands" implies, this is an area dominated by grass, whether that is tall, short, or a mix of both. Naturally, it's much easier for a predator to hide in tall grass. And, therefore, we may be tempted to use this quite often. After all, we can have something hiding that is trying to attack our characters.

However, it is tempting to do this everywhere so that we have that possibility everywhere, but if you're creating a setting for a particular story, decide whether you need this or not. And, if you don't, then go ahead with the short grass, just because there are probably going to be opportunities for you to use taller grasslands in another story. And we don't want to get into a habit of always making them tall. So, if you don't need them to be tall, just go ahead and make them short.

We've probably all seen TV shows or movies where our characters, or something that's after them, is using the tall grass to their advantage. This is a pretty good hiding spot, with one exception. If you are already being pursued and you enter these grasslands, you're going to leave a trail that's going to last for a little while. And, therefore, it's going to be relatively easy for whatever's following you to follow that trail.

But, otherwise, if more time has passed, you can easily hide in these tall grasses for a long time. To some extent, that will depend upon your predator because if they have a good sense of smell, then they may be able to follow you anyway. But, for those of us, like humans, who are mostly going by sight, we are at a disadvantage trying to find someone who has been in those grasslands for a while.

That said, we've all seen characters who are good at tracking, which is identifying how the ground has been disturbed, or how vegetation has been disturbed. And, therefore, following the path. So, this is another option to give our human characters, or others who are like them, the ability to track someone anyway. Of course, if there is aerial pursuit, then this isn't going to work nearly as well.

Now, if you're wondering where the taller grass is more likely to occur, the answer should be fairly obvious. It's going to be where there is more rain. This is something to keep in mind beyond your story needs because if you have a desert and you would like the characters to run right out of that desert into tall grass, that's probably not going to happen because the whole reason there is a desert there is that there's not a lot of precipitation. And, therefore, it doesn't make too much sense that there's going to be tall grass right next to it anymore than there would be a forest right there. What is realistic is that we would have short grass that slowly gives way to taller and taller grass and, eventually, to a forest.

Something else to be aware of is that in tropic climates near the equator, sometimes almost all of the year's rain happen in just a couple weeks. This might mean that those tall, green grasslands are only a temporary feature.

I've mentioned the issue of prevailing winds and rain shadows, and how mountains can affect rainfall, and I'm going to do so again here using the United States as an example. When the Rocky Mountains rose out west, what happened is that this caused a rain shadow that killed the forest for hundreds of miles to the Midwest. And this caused the famous plains that are dominating the Midwest.

The reason this happened is that those mountains caused most of the water to come out of the clouds, into the mountains, and then, on the other side, there wasn't any moisture to fall – or not enough to cause more lush vegetation. This is still true today, but when I did some research on this, one of the things I found is that the Native Americans would periodically burn down the grasslands, and they were doing this for a specific reason. They were trying to prevent trees from growing there because, eventually, those trees would start to grow and they would start to become a savanna, which we talked about in the previous episode. And, in time, a savannah could start to become a woodland, which has more trees, and then it could eventually become a forest. And they did not want this. They wanted more land for their livestock to graze.

So, they periodically burned all the grasslands down. Well, not all of them, obviously, but they would set fires that would burn for many miles and this would kill off any potential trees that were starting to grow.

One thing this shows us is that even before modern civilization, humans had the ability to manipulate the land. So, if you have a world in a fantasy setting where there is not modern technology, your people could still be causing such a thing to happen. In fact, if we're going to create a story that happens on a plain and have our characters get involved with nomads, for example, we might actually want to show a scene of them burning down the grasslands. Or we can just have our characters come across an area that has been burned, and maybe they think it's natural, like a lightning strike, but it actually isn't.

On that note, when we create grasslands, we shouldn't decide that there's no population there, but we might want to go ahead and decide that there are nomads populating it. Not only is this reasonable, but it gives our characters someone that they might run across while they're traveling. The nomadic culture is going to be very different from the culture of people who live in cities, and this gives us a good opportunity to show some more variety. These nomads might also be hostile or friendly depending on their relationship with those in the city. After all, there is likely to be some trade going on, but there might also be some suspicion on both sides, and possibly some past conflicts. So this, again, gives us more diversity and some history.

This is more likely anytime we have a wide expanse of land that is full of grasslands. So, if you have an especially tall group of mountains in the interior of a continent – which, as we learned in a previous episode, is where the tallest mountains will be – then we just need to know which direction the prevailing winds are going based on how far this land mass or this mountain range is from the equator, and then we can decide that on one side of this there is heavy forest, and on the other side there are many miles of grasslands that are populated by nomadic tribes.

DESERTS

While we're talking about areas with limited rainfall, let's talk about deserts. It may surprise you to know that, here on Earth, deserts take up an entire third of the land surface. Not the entire surface, just the surface covered by land. So, don't be shy about placing deserts on your world because they're definitely going to be there, although we can change how many deserts are on the world.

However, you may want to not stray too far from doing a third of the land surface, and there's a reason for this. The deserts play a role in regulating the planet's temperature. So, if we go far outside of that, we may be messing with how things work. Although, the average person is not going to know this. Still, it's something to keep in mind and follows that idea to know the rules before you break them. So, don't be shy about adding deserts in many places.

And the obvious question is where would they form? And, if you've been listening to this and the previous ones, the obvious answer is that they would form to one side of a mountain range. This isn't always true, but it often is. On that note, some deserts do receive rain, but they don't receive enough to compensate for the high levels of evaporation. How little rain to we need in a year to cause a desert? Just 10 inches, which is really not that much.

Don't think of a desert as a place where it never rains, because that's usually not true. Some places are sort of semi-deserts because they receive 10 to 20 inches of rain, and some of these also have grass, in which case it's called a steppe. So, this will be a place where it is still fairly barren, but not nearly as barren as a place with bare rock or sand. Once again, this variation keeps us from having everywhere be the same. Land that is closet to a mountain range might be a desert because of the lack of rainfall that the rain shadow caused, whereas land that is a little bit further away might be a steppe because it's getting a little bit more rainfall and, therefore, has low grass. That, in turn, might give way to actual grasslands.

Of course, the reason that there is increasing vegetation further and further away from that rain shadow desert is that there is moisture in the air that is being picked up continuously. It's just that most of it that was in the air before it hit the mountain range left those clouds. By the way, when it does rain in the desert, it often happens in a violent downpour, and this can cause a flash flood that happens miles away from where the storm actually is.

Another interesting fact about deserts is that they normally cannot form too close to the equator because there is too much heavy rain in the tropics from 0°, which is the equator, up to a roughly 30° latitude. That said, it is possible to have a desert here, and you may be able to guess why. There are areas near the equator where the elevation is very high and, as a result, instead of it being a tropical climate there, it's actually a more temperate climate that would normally be found further north or south, away from the equator. The result is that if there are mountains there, there can actually be a rain shadow. And, as a result of that, an actual desert that is at the equator.

When it comes to the composition of deserts, it might also surprise you to know that only 20% of the Earth's deserts are actually made of sand. Hollywood tends to show us this as the default, so most of us probably assume that's how all of them are. But it's not true. This is yet another way that we can make one desert different from another.

The rest of the deserts are actually kind of like a virtual pavement of tightly packed small stones like pebbles. Hearing me say that, you might assume that it's very loose, but it's actually very stable. This hard desert is hard on the feet, including those of animals.

One thing that this also means is that people can move relatively quickly through this, as opposed to a sandy desert. So, while a horse might struggle in sand, it will be fine on the hard desert. However, the hard desert is actually going to hurt its hooves. That doesn't mean that the horse can't travel on it, it just means that sooner or later it's going to get fatigued, and that's probably going to happen sooner. Horses prefer relatively soft earth, but not so soft that it's like mud. So, when you're working on your travel times, consider what type of desert is in a specific place.

So, the question then becomes where do you find a sandy desert versus a hard desert? One answer to this is to understand why sand forms. Basically, what's happening is that extreme temperature changes from day to night cause rocks to break apart. After that, more erosion occurs from wind, and you end up with sand. In an earlier episode, we talked about climates, including the dry climate, and this is where deserts are typically found. Both the hot and the cold deserts are more likely to have this, as opposed to the mild deserts where the temperatures are not that extreme.

While there are a few more little details in the *Creating Places* book, the last thing I want to mention about deserts is the difference between a sandstorm and a dust storm, as these are not the same thing. Most of us have probably seen these towering images of what looks like a sandstorm engulfing an entire city, while these are actually dust storms. Sand is too heavy to get that high into the air. In fact, it doesn't get much higher than us. What sand will do is pelt you sideways. It does not actually fall down on us from above, because it's not going to get that high.

So, a dust storm looks really impressive, but is it really that lethal? And the answer is, actually, yes, because exposure to dust storms, if it happens repeatedly, can actually cause an incurable respiratory illness. Now, that can cause people to eventually suffocate. This does not sound as exciting or as dangerous as immediate death from sandstorms, but a dust storm is actually more likely to cause death. If we're going to be writing a story that features one of these storms, we should have some idea of the difference here and use it appropriately.

WETLANDS

Now that we've talked about places with very little water, let's talk about places with so much so that they are called wetlands. As it turns out, a wetland can either be freshwater, saltwater or brackish, which means that it is somewhere in between. Not surprisingly, the freshwater ones tend to be inland where water is coming from rainfall and runoff, whereas on the coast we're more likely to have the saltwater ones. The ones that are brackish are still going to be near the coast, since that's where the saltwater is coming from, but they also have a freshwater source, which is either going to be rain or a nearby lake, or a river, or possibly an underground spring. The result is called brackish.

As storytellers, we can use wetlands as a place where monsters like to hide because humans, in particular, tend to like solid ground and not be that comfortable going into them. Those who spend a lot of time in wetlands will feel differently, of course. These might also be the people who are familiar with that monster or what it is capable of, and even where it tends to be. They are likely to be the source of rumors about it, too, whether those prove to be true or false. Most wetlands are found in the temperate climate zone or in the tropics near the equator, but they can be in polar areas, too.

When it comes to the freshwater wetlands, what we might want to do is decide that there is an area of any lake that is actually a wetland. This could be any side of it, and what we're talking about is a transition from lake to solid ground. And that area in between is going to be our wetland. This is generally the case. So, we don't need to invent new areas on our map if we've got one. We can just decide that one area of a lake is the wetland.

Aside from monsters, why would we want to create one? Well, there could be lots of fish and other animals that have this as their habitat, and this results in products and other things that our characters might be using, which also includes food. In a world with magic, we could certainly decide that some sort of plant is growing there, and that it is very valuable, and that's the only kind of place it's found. And, therefore, those who are comfortable moving around in that wetland are going to be the ones who are harvesting that. And, therefore, they might have some position of prominence, at least when it comes to that particular item. Now, if it turns out that we do have a monster and we have that special plant there, maybe the monster has some sort of special property as a result of having access to that plant.

MIRES

There are four types of wetlands, and the first two are both known as mires. This includes bogs and fens. After that, we're going to talk about marshes and then swamps.

When it comes to bogs and fens, both types of mires get their water from rainfall. Both of them form at the edges of lakes, as we were just talking about, and sometimes they can even cover the entire surface of that lake. So, what's the difference between a bog and a fen? Let's talk about bogs first.

A bog forms in a low area of land or on top of an old lake, which also forms in a low area of land. A bog can be many meters deep, and what happens on the surface is that dead plant material, like mosses, tends to form peat. Evergreen plants can grow on the surface, and one of the things that can happen is that, from a distance, it might look like it is just regular land and you might have no idea that there is actually water under there. This is especially true if it happens to be adjacent to a forest and, therefore, it just looks like the ground blends right into the forest in the background. And so, you could have a scene where a group of warriors on horseback are charging across the land, and they think they're heading for that forest, having no idea that there's actually a peat bog there and they're just going to tumble right into the water.

One interesting idea we can leverage is that sometimes carnivorous plants exist in bogs, and these survive by eating invertebrate, but there's no reason we can't have bigger plants that survive by eating our people. In drier locations, we can actually have trees growing in these bogs. So, it's not impossible to have a large plant. And by large, I don't necessarily mean that it's tall because a plant could be many meters across, lying across this apparent ground, which is actually peat.

Sometimes on Earth, large animals, like moose and caribou, are found in bogs, and there are a lot of other animals like otters and just smaller animals that use this as their home. And then the peat moss itself can be used as fuel for either heating or cooking. This, once again, gives us a product that we can mention in our city if there's a nearby lake that has a bog on one end of it. Maybe someone is burning peat moss for fuel.

So, how does all of this differ from a fen? And the answer is pretty simple. Instead of being covered in peat, a fen is covered in grasses and shrubs. In addition to occurring along lakes, they can also occur alongside a river. They also typically get most of their water from the ground rather than rain, but this is not the kind of difference that your audience is likely to notice or care about if you point it out to them. A fen can also turn into a bog in time. Like bogs, fens have a tendency to be found in the mountains. And, just like with bogs, they can be deceptive from a distance so that you don't realize it's a fen and you might just assume it's a grassland.

MARSHES

Let's talk about another type of wetland, a marsh. They also form in a depression of land, or at the edge of a lake, or along the side of a slow-moving river. The water tends to be shallower here. Keep this in mind if you're intending to use a marsh as the habitat of a large water-dwelling animal because that may not make as much sense as placing that into a bog or a fen, for example. The monster that we were discussing earlier is probably going to be more a land-dweller than a water-dweller if it calls a marsh its home. But, as for other life here, we can still have fish, bird, amphibians and smaller aquatic mammals. Instead of grasses and trees, like you would find in a fen, or the peat that you would find in a bog, here we would have grasses and reeds.

It is possible to have a saltwater marsh. These are found further from the equator along a coastline where the tide will flood them. However, they must usually be protected by a lagoon or an estuary because, otherwise, the flow of water coming in and out might be too strong.

SWAMPS

And that brings us to the last wetland, and that is the swamp. This is one that we've all heard about, but we may not understand the difference between this and other types of wetlands. It's basically a wetland that is a forest, meaning there are a lot of trees here. One way this is different from a fen is that fens don't have nearly as many trees. As you might expect, a swamp occurs near large rivers and lakes. This means that we can once again take any lake that's on our map and decide that part of it is a swamp. This swamp might also connect directly to an actual forest where the ground is solid.

Now, it is possible to have two different types of swamp, one of them being a swamp forest, and one of them being a brush swamp. And the difference is the amount of tree cover. The shrub version has fewer and shorter trees and is mostly bushes instead.

Now, within a swamp, there are sometimes dry areas of land that are raised, and these are called a hammock. This is where the shrubs tend to be found.

In a fantasy world, we know that elves love forests, but there seems to be not much mention of elves loving a swamp, though this is just a forest with a lot of water. But maybe this is something that we can exploit in our world. Surely, the elves can find a use for this particular habitat.

Now, that said, we often show elves as living up in extremely tall trees, and it's possible that such tall trees are not going to be growing inside a swamp for the simple reason that the ground is so saturated that they may not be able to grow that tall without falling over. Maybe this is the reason we don't talk about elves being in swamps.

However, while they may not live in the swamp, there are certainly going to be times when there is a forest, and there's a lake, and in between there is a swamp. And I see no reason why we can't have elves make use of that swamp. At the very least, they're going to be familiar with the types of creatures that live within it. They might turn them into products or have other uses for them, and this is something that we should explore as world builders.

So, that about wraps up Chapter 4, "Creating Land Features," although I do have a few sections in the book that I'm not going to cover here, including settlements, which is briefly talked about in relation to these land features, and then the cultivation, meaning how much the humans and other species have manipulated this land for their benefit, and the impact that this can have on that settlement and the corresponding land features.

HOW TO CREATE
SOVEREIGN POWERS

Hello and welcome to *The Art of World Building Podcast*, episode number fourteen, part 1. Today's topic is how to create sovereign powers like kingdoms, dictatorships, republics, and more. This includes what sovereignty is, how it is gained and lost, the divine right of kings, some roles like head of state and what each means, and branches of government. This material and more is discussed in chapter 7 of *Creating Places*, volume 2 in *The Art of World Building* book series.

WHAT IS SOVEREIGNTY?

To talk about sovereignty, we naturally need to understand what sovereignty means. Basically, it's the right to govern oneself without outside interference. It's also a question of recognition, both from other countries and from the people within its borders. This is known as external sovereignty versus internal sovereignty. We'll talk about both of these in more detail now.

External Sovereignty

A sovereign power may or may not be recognized as having sovereignty by other powers. In other words, we can't just buy an island somewhere, declare ourselves the king and have sovereignty because other, actual sovereign powers may refuse to recognize that we have this sovereignty. There are some reasons why they may refuse to do so.

Exclusivity is one of these reasons. If two sovereign powers are contesting an area of land, that means that neither of them is recognizing that the other one has sovereignty over that land. Therefore, neither of them have sovereignty. Of course, a power could have sovereignty over other lands where that is recognized, but when it tries to take over another area of land, its sovereignty over that particular area is not recognized.

There is a modern example of this where Russia has sovereignty over many lands, and there was another country that was independent and had sovereignty, but Russia decided that because its citizens lived in that country, that this other country belonged to it. So, it invaded and took over that country. And it felt that it had the right to do so, but most of the rest of the world disagreed. In this instance, what Russia was doing was claiming that it had sovereignty over that country and, at the same time, it refused to recognize that that country had any sovereignty of its own. Since much of the rest of the world, such as the European Union, did not agree with this, Russia was subsequently punished and kicked out of the G8 summit, which became the G7 as a result.

So, if two powers are claiming sovereignty over something, or somewhere, then one of those sovereign powers must be destroyed, or it must be engulfed by the other, or otherwise proven illegitimate. Otherwise, neither of them is truly sovereign. Two powers cannot be sovereign over the same territory. One of them has to give.

Another factor that can come up is that sometimes a sovereign has the legal right to control a territory, but it doesn't have that actual control due to a lack of military. Their military may be insufficient to control that territory. This is something that comes up in war when one country attacks another and drives them out, but other countries see the invaders as exactly that – they are invaders who do not actually have a sovereign claim to that territory. Sometimes, when the war is finally over, it's because allies have kicked out that invading country on behalf of the country that was invaded.

I said that in a way that's a little bit confusing, so let's use an example. This may not be historically accurate, but let's say that Germany invaded France and expelled the French nobility so that they were no longer there, but the rest of the world did not recognize that Germany now had sovereignty over France. The rest of the world might have thought France has been invaded and they need to be properly put back where they belong when it comes to the rulers. So, therefore, French allies might have joined forces with France and helped expel the Germans. In this case, the reason for this was the question of sovereignty. France's sovereignty over that territory was recognized by other countries, but Germany's claim on sovereignty over French territory was not respected.

During this war, it's possible that France's army would've been defeated. And, in that sense, it would have this legal right over that territory, but no longer have the military might to enforce that sovereignty. Therefore, it would have to turn to allies to help it. If those allies agreed, then they would help. If they did not agree, then Germany would be successful in taking over that territory. Now, just because Germany has taken over France, that doesn't mean that other countries immediately recognize that it has sovereignty over France, but, in time, they may.

Now, rather than this being a military issue, there could be other reasons such as a population that is being uncooperative. Perhaps Germany is trying to rule France, but the French citizens are just being incredibly difficult and rebelling all the time. This could make it difficult for Germany to exert the sovereignty that it is trying to claim, even if Germany has defeated France's military.

We'll be talking about internal sovereignty in a few minutes, but, basically, that's what we're hinting at here. If Germany now possesses France's territory, but the citizens of France do not recognize that they are now citizens of Germany, then there's a bit of a problem. The territory itself, the people in it, are not recognizing Germany's claim of sovereignty.

It's also possible to achieve sovereignty but not be independent due to needing help from other powers. In fantasy and science fiction, we probably don't like this idea because we want someone who is weak to be overtaken by a nefarious kingdom that our heroes can then try to destroy. So, if a kingdom has sovereignty but it needs a lot of help and is, therefore, not independent, it could be taken advantage of by another sovereign power. Or, in the case of our fantasy and sci-fi settings where we want more aggression, then it could just be taken over.

But there are times when a large country, like the United States, is benevolent toward other countries and trying to stand them up as a democracy, for example. One of the reasons that can happen is for ideological reasons where we prefer democracy to spread throughout the world as opposed to authoritarian governments proliferating. Therefore, if there is what we consider to be an evil regime that has fallen, and a new government hasn't taken its place yet, but they show an interest in democracy, we might help them try to achieve that democracy. In this case, what we would be doing is showing them respect for their culture and their own sovereignty. And, even though they need help from us, we are providing that without just trying to take them over.

The kind of assistance that one power can lend another could be military, it could be technological – which is especially interesting in science fiction – or it could be humanitarian. Or, in fantasy settings, it could be magical assistance. Maybe the wizards of that sovereign power don't have anywhere they can get schooling, so we allow them to come to our country for that. The same could be said for the ability to pilot spacecraft. Maybe they don't have the training facilities, but they've got people who have the talent. So, we provide that for them. We give them the training. Maybe we even loan them some ships or help them start their own industry. The leader of such a sovereign power, such as a monarch, might want military aid that he has to bargain for by offering something else, such as crops or natural resources.

One thing that we can gain from all of this as world builders is that we can start thinking of alliances that different sovereign powers might have because of the ability to trade for something that they don't have in their territory. So, for example, if your sovereign power has no large forests, then they're going to be at a loss for the kind of wood that might be needed to build wooden ships if we're in a fantasy setting. A sovereign power that has no mountains might have a lack of mines and, therefore, no ore to build technological weapons or spacecraft. This is one way that the terrain of a sovereign power can be used to help us create more relationships that make sense.

INTERNAL SOVEREIGNTY

Now we should talk about internal sovereignty, which is whether the sovereign power is recognized by its own subjects. In more extreme cases, people might overthrow the ruler, or murder him, imprison him or even exile him. As storytellers, we tend to like these more extreme versions, don't we? If the person who has been overthrown still lives because they've been exiled or imprisoned, that does give us the option for further problems that this person could cause. Death tends to eliminate that option unless we have a setting where undead are an option.

So, the obvious question is when does a ruler get overthrown by his people? Why do they not respect his sovereignty? The main answer for that is weakness or, at least, perceived weakness. This can come in several ways. The inability to create peace, or restore it if it has been disrupted, is one of the reasons. War is not typically good for anyone. Though, in our modern times, we sometimes cynically say that the companies who manufacture weapons, for example, often benefit from war. And that is true, but, generally speaking, war is devastating, and it's considered a very negative thing.

This is still true even if your side wins. The reason people celebrate the end of a war is that they can go back to their peaceful lives. So, a ruler who cannot create peace or restore it when something has gone wrong is considered weak, and he might end up getting overthrown if the tension goes on for too long. It also must be remembered that

usually it is males who get sent into war – at least historically on Earth – and this really does cause a major problem
with reproduction and people's ancestry continuing as
people are being killed off during battles. If war drags on
for a long time, this can really have a devastating affect on
many aspects of life. But it's not even just war. Even smaller conflicts can cause these kinds of problems.

Another source of peace going wrong could be rebel-
lions. If there is one happening within the country, and the
ruler is unable to squash this, this can be considered weak.
That tends to encourage more people to rebel, so this tends
to be bad for not only the ruler, but the people who are
trusting him to do something about this will increasingly
lose faith. And they might actually join such a rebellion.

Another potential sign of weakness is when the ruler
refuses to enforce a law when those laws are being broken
in a way that are very costly to the country. For example,
in the United States and other countries, we have immigration laws. There are people who feel like illegal immigration is a major problem and the government is not doing
enough to enforce the laws by removing illegal immigrants.
The failure to act in a way that the people find acceptable
is considered a sign of weakness.

Of course, another issue is that a leader could be too
strong about enforcing those laws in such a way that it is
disrespectful of human rights, and that this also causes
disillusionment and an idea that the leader is still being
weak because they are actually being too forceful in the
name of being strong. But, you know, being strong doesn't
mean being cruel to people, such as separating children
from their parents when they cross a border illegally because of your detention policies.

So, different people are going to have different ideas
about that, but this is a very timely subject. This is an issue
that's not only happening in the United States right now,

but in other countries, due to an unusual amount of migrant population moving from one country to another, not only in the United States, but also in Europe. So, this is an example of a law that is not being enforced enough for some people who have determined that the leader is, therefore, weak. They, therefore, lose respect for that leader. Incidentally, enforcing laws in a draconian fashion might also upset the people so that the rebel.

Something else that we also see play out in our own country is that promises to one's own people need to be kept. We often see people being removed from office in democracies because the people feel like they campaigned on certain promises and then did not uphold them once they were elected. So, at the next election, they get booted out of office. In our science fiction and fantasy settings, we might especially want to pay attention to the idea that promises that are made to one's own police force and military force must be kept. Otherwise, this can result in an internal war and a coup with a military junta or dictatorship taking the place of whatever leadership was there. And if you're not sure what a military junta is, we're going to be talking about that in another episode.

And the last note on this is that many centuries ago, people tended to believe that a single person should rule because this provided a single voice of decisions. But, as the years have passed, this idea has slowly fallen out of favor. We've moved towards more countries that have an elected body, such as a parliament, that has authority.

GAINING SOVEREIGNTY

All of this may have you wondering how a power gains sovereignty. So, let's talk about that. As I alluded to earlier, a conquest is one of the more interesting reasons for us. In the modern world, and potentially in science fiction settings where there is a lot of communication, there might be more of this issue that we have today where things like the European Union are joined. These are multiple countries that are working together. And, therefore, at this point in Earth's history, we are generally opposed to one country conquering another.

While that may have been true in the past, the military might that we had back then was not so great, and the cooperation was not so great that we could actually stop countries from doing this as much as we can today. One of the reasons we can stop countries from doing this is that we have a very integrated world when it comes to things like trade, and we can jointly punish a country that invades another, the same way that Russia was recently punished.

So, if we are creating a setting that is like that, this is something to consider. We might not have sovereign powers conquering each other so much anymore. But, if we've got a setting that is more like what you typically see in fantasy, then it's much easier for one country to simply attack and absorb another, and then hold onto that territory for long enough that it is considered sovereign over that territory. How long is long enough? Well, it's probably going to be at least 5 years, maybe 10. But, certainly after 100 years, everyone who was alive when it used to be another sovereign power is now dead, unless we have something like elves that live 1,000 years or more.

So, if no one in living memory even remembers that being a different kingdom, then it's no longer that kingdom. That's gone. That kingdom might actually still exist, but the territory that it used to have might have been taken over by another country and held for so long that it is considered part of that other country. Although, of course, we could still have historical records and people saying,

"Okay. This is still a sore point. We still want that area back." But it might have gotten to the point where other countries just decide, "Okay. We recognize that this other sovereign power has taken over that country or that territory for so long and has held onto it that we now recognize, yes, it is sovereign over that territory."

Another possibility that can come up is that one power could cede land to another via a treaty, for example. This isn't the most exciting for us, but it does happen. An example of this would be the Louisiana Purchase that happened in the United States where the United States bought a huge territory in the center of the United States, or what is now the center of the U.S., from, I believe, France. And why did France agree to sell that huge area of land? Well, France was having a money issue back in France because Napoleon had declared war and was attacking all these different other sovereign powers. He also decided he couldn't fight wars over there and over here at the same time, so he just sold the territory to the United States. Now, it's been a while since I read about that, so there may be details I'm forgetting, but you get the basic idea.

There's another way that territory can be claimed, and that is if no one is claiming sovereignty over it, then, in a sense, it is up for grabs. The example I'm going to use is, once again, the United States because when the Europeans – the British, the French, and the Spanish conquerors – landed on what is now United States territory, each one of them just claimed sovereignty over different areas of it. Why did they feel that they could do this? The Native Americans were here. The answer is that the Native Americans did not really understand this concept of sovereignty, and they didn't recognize it. And, therefore, they weren't really sovereign over this territory. They considered it to belong to everyone. You know, these other people come in and decide, "Well, no. This belongs to my country. That belongs to the other one." So, it just got divided up.

Basically, these countries that invaded did not recognize any sovereignty by the Native Americans. And, therefore, they just took the land. There were overlaps, at times, with different countries claiming different areas of that land. And, of course, that led to wars and, eventually, what is now the United States won out and everyone else ended up leaving. When other countries departed, what they were doing was also finally, and formally, recognizing that the United States had sovereignty over that land.

We can use this same sort of scenario, especially in science fiction, where different spaceships from different planets or sovereign powers could discover a country at roughly the same time. And they start investigating the minerals and other ores that this planet provides, and different countries could be deciding that they want one continent, or part of it, versus another one. And, next thing you know, you have all these wars. You know, I haven't seen this scenario played out in a science fiction book, but it seems like something that's fairly obvious. This might be a little bit harder to do in fantasy, unless we have a situation very similar to the one I described a minute ago about the Native Americans. Of course, what precipitated that was an improvement in the quality of ships that could sail over the open ocean. And, therefore, different countries were able to discover North America at roughly the same time. By roughly, I mean over the span of a couple decades.

Barring something like that in a fantasy setting, we might have to have something like the wall in *Game of Thrones* come down, and various kingdoms decide that they want to take that land. There would have to be some sort of discovery of new land that no one had claimed in order for several countries to rush in and start claiming it.

THE DIVINE RIGHT OF KINGS

Let's also talk about the divine right of kings. This is something that sounds really cool, and which you've probably heard of before. Basically, what this means on Earth is that someone is considered to be sovereign by the will of god, and that is the only person to whom they answer. A dictator or an absolute monarch is going to be viewed this way, or, at least, want others to view them this way. It implies that they are above the law.

You've probably also heard that quote that absolute power corrupts absolutely. So, tyrants tend to like this idea. It could be considered treasonous to stand in the way of this absolute monarch. If we have a world where there is more than one god, we could also do this and have one person decide that they were appointed by one god to be the ruler, and another person could decide that they were the one appointed by a different god to be the ruler, so that we could have conflict.

Now, here on Earth, some places, like Asia, consider a sovereign to be legitimate only if he is a just ruler. If he is unjust and engages in bad behavior, then he could be stripped of sovereignty. This is an area ripe for conflict because we could have some people deciding that this sovereign was acting justly, while other people decide he was unjust. And, therefore, when he is stripped of power, some people might want him to be restored to power. So, this is another way we can use something for storytelling.

LOSING SOVEREIGNTY

Since we've talked about gaining sovereignty, let's talk about losing it. We've already touched upon this because one of the most obvious ways is to be conquered. Another is to be overthrown from within, such as during the French and American Revolutions. Both of these violently ended the rule of sovereign powers. When this happens, a new government must take its place. If you're looking for ideas on what sort of government could replace them, we will be covering many options in the next episode. There are some additional details found in Chapter 5 of *Creating Places*, but I'm going to move onto roles such as the head of state and head of government next.

HEAD OF STATE

The head of state and head of government are the two most important roles in a government. And, at first glance, this might sound like it's going to be a boring subject, but it can actually be really interesting and very beneficial to understand this when we are doing world building or any storytelling involving these characters.

The head of state is the visible representative of a sovereign power. He may have no actual power, or very limited powers, being largely ceremonial. This is the monarch who might show up to bless a battleship or a sailing vessel, or to knight someone. If there's an annual parade on a big holiday, this is the figurehead who will be in a prominent position during that parade. Sometimes, they appear to have power, but they are just going through the motions. That could be something like signing a bill into law where the parliament actually does that, but this person still signs off on it. This head of state is also the highest military leader, or commander in chief, but, as with other subjects, this power could actually be ceded to other people who have control of it.

Examples of heads of state would be kings, emperors and presidents. A president is sworn in, whereas a coronation is for a monarch. As world builders, we have the ability to grant these heads of state whatever powers we would like them to have. On Earth, this changes from kingdom to kingdom, so we can do whatever we want here. Don't feel like you have to get this right by modeling it on some kingdom here on Earth.

We also don't have to explain the reasons why they are only ceremonial, in one way or another, and have no actual power. Readers don't typically want some sort of history lesson unless that story has something to do with the reason this character does not have the power, because that character wants to flex that power and discovers they don't have it. Unless it's part of your story, you don't need to worry about that too much.

HEAD OF GOVERNMENT

The more important role, arguably, is the head of government. This person is the one leading government, and they usually have a title such as prime minister or chancellor. If this person is also the head of state, then they will have a title like king, emperor or president. Arguably, writers tend to simply give a title like "President So-and-so" without actually explaining anything about what they can do. Some of that may be natural because we don't really want to bore the audience with exposition explaining all the things that they can and cannot do, especially if they're not going to impact our story. But it does help us to think about this. So, I'm going to give you a couple ideas here.

What we want to do is think about what this head of government can actually do. So, for example, can they veto laws or sign them into existence by themselves, or do they need parliament? Can they be removed from office, and by who? Are they protected from prosecution? Can they be executed? Can they raise and lower taxes? Do they need permission or cooperation from others in government to get anything done? Can they declare war? Are there exceptions to any of this? For example, maybe they cannot declare war under normal circumstances, but, in more extreme ones, they can.

If our sovereign power has a prime minister who is head of government, that means there is also a ceremonial head of state who has less power. An example of this would be the prime minster of Great Britain. He is the actual head of government. The queen is the ceremonial head of state. This is why the President of the United States meets with the Prime Minister of Britain to discuss matters of government, because these are the two heads of government. Now, in the case of the United States, the president is also the head of state. So, there are times when, in the capacity of head of state, the President of the United States meets with the Queen of England, but this is mostly a ceremonial function. Why is that? Because the Queen of England does not have that much power. All of that resides with the prime minister and with the parliament.

And if you were paying attention, I did just say that in something like the United States, which is a democracy, one person is in the role of head of state and head of government. But then, in certain other setups, like a monarchy, we might have the king or queen be the head of state. Power has been ceded to the prime minister and parliament. This is what's known as a constitutional monarchy, and we'll be talking about that more and it's alternate version, the absolute monarchy, in the next episode. The absolute monarchy is one where the king is the head of government and the head of state.

BRANCHES OF GOVERNMENT

I'm going to talk about the different branches of government. The executive branch is the one that administers the state and enforces the laws which are passed by the legislative branch, whereas the judicial branch is the one that interprets those laws. The reason this is separated this way is to prevent abuse of power. Even in a democracy, there are those who wish to abuse power and try to merge or force their way past these delineations to get what they want. The separation of powers inhibits that. It is built into the government structure by design and on purpose to prevent the sort of abuses that happened in the past.

An absolute monarchy where the king is both head of state and head of government, and believes he has this divine right of kings and only answers to god, this king is the kind of guy who's going to do tyrannical things that really upset a lot of people. And, over time, people resisted this kind of thing. Sometimes, they got executed by the king for this. But, sometimes, enough resistance built up in the population that the king ended up having no choice but to cede power to government, and he became a head of state and, next thing you know, you had a parliament that had these different branches of government. And that parliament was led by the prime minister who was the head of government who had much of the power.

One thing that we are implying here is that earlier forms of government were often this type where they were an absolute monarchy, and things have progressively moved toward a more diverse separation of powers so that no one person has that much control. One way we can use this in our world building is that if we have a very advanced society that you're likely to see in science fiction, then they may have also moved away from things like absolute monarchies. On the other hand, a fantasy setting where things tend to be more like our past, like a medieval setting, they are more prone to having this sort of government because, maybe, they have not collectively moved past it. By collectively, I mean that multiple countries might still have monarchies. On Earth, this was once the primary form of government, or one of them, and today, it is one of the least popular or common ones.

HOW TO CREATE
SOVEREIGN POWERS

Hello and welcome to *The Art of World Building Podcast*, episode number fourteen, part two. Today's topic is how create sovereign powers by understanding government types like federations, unitary states, kingdoms, dictatorships, authoritarian states, oligarchies, republics, and more, including how they rise and fall. This material and more is discussed in chapter 5 of *Creating Places*, volume 2 in *The Art of World Building* book series.

GOVERNMENT TYPES

Most of us probably think that a subject like government types is going to be kind of dry, and maybe a little bit boring, but I have found that it's actually one of the more interesting subjects when it comes to building a world, and even creating a setting for our stories where it can impact the story that we are telling. One reason we might think it's not interesting is that we just don't know some of these things. And so, one government type is kind of the same as another to us, unless we have looked into this or we've recently taken something like a high school or college course on the subject.

You could do a lot of research on this, but one of the things that I've done with this entire series is done that research for you. Now, I won't cover absolutely everything because there are literally entire books written about government types. And, in fact, they're probably entire books written about one specific government type, such as a monarchy. But what I have done is collected all of what I feel are the relevant, high-level details about what we need to know as world builders. And that's part of what we're going to discuss today.

If you really do want extreme detail because you're going to write a story kind of like *Game of Thrones*, where the details of how government works actually matter to your story, there are many resources out there that you can find. But, for most of us, we are really just trying to decide what the government is like because of how this affects life for our characters. And we really only want a high level of detail on this. So, that's what I'm going to cover here. It's not because I'm lazy or I don't find it interesting. It's partly because I'm trying to teach and reach the widest audience here. One thing I'm hoping that may happen for you is that you become more interested in this and then you go ahead and do the deeper dive into it on your own.

In quite a few episodes, I've talked about using analogues, which is basically when we invent something that is based on something here on Earth. Government types is a good way of doing this and we can even use things that have happened with governments here on Earth to model something on. For example, in recent times, the government of Somalia has kind of fallen apart and been destabilized and, as a result, pirates have sought a better life through attacking ships that are sailing near. And this is something that we can use ourselves.

If that seems like it's too recent an example and some-one, a reader of yours, may realize what you're basing it on, then you can look through Wikipedia on any country and find things that have happened in that country's histo-ry when one government type or another fell, or rose, and different things that happened within that country. We can take one of these, modify it a little bit, and it'll be some-thing of our own. This is also a good way to get ideas.

On that note, with *Game of Thrones*, George R.R. Mar-tin did not invent much of what is there. He's based it on real life events in England. Now, this is not taking anything away from him because he has admitted this and it's basi-cally a point of inspiration. It's funny how if you plagiarize someone's words, people have a big issue with that, but if you take an idea like what happened in England and then turn it into a book series, like *Game of Thrones*, people will actually appreciate the fact that you've called their atten-tion to something that happened in history. So, it's not only not considered bad, but it can actually be considered a plus and you can be given more esteem because you have taken something from the real world and turned it into an intelligent story. So, don't be afraid to use an analogue.

Something else I should mention at the start here is that sometimes a country has a name that is misleading and is actually wrong. For example, we could call something the Empire of Kysh when it's really a federation if we looked at how it's government works. But maybe the peo-ple in that country decided it sounded better to call them-selves an empire. This is not a scenario that I am making up. This is something that actually happens here on Earth. So, as world builders, we should try to use the correct name for something, but we can get away with using the wrong name. It's just one of those situations where you should know the rule before you break it because there's always going to be that guy who comes along and says, "Hey, that's incorrect. You're using the wrong name. You don't know what you're doing." Well, make sure that you do know what you're doing, and then, if you're using the wrong name, do it on purpose, for a reason. And it can be as simple a reason as I like the way that *sounds*.

Something else to bear in mind — and this is something that can really enrich our world — is that no government type lasts forever. Now, if it's relatively young, such as a couple decades, then maybe it does. But in the case of something that's been around a thousand years, most likely the form of government has changed repeatedly. And it can go kind of in any order. We've got all these different options like a constitutional monarchy, an absolute monarchy, a dictatorship, a federation.

So, these things change. We'll talk a little bit as we go along about how things can change from one type of government to another. This is something that can make our setting a little more interesting, and certainly the story that we're telling somewhere, because any government type that came and went is going to leave some sort of impact. And it could be just something like a dictatorship creating these hulking, brutish buildings that are intimidating to people, and that architecture still being around.

The type of money that is around, or some of the laws, could come from a previous government type and still be considered just part of the way things are now, even though there's a new government type. Obviously, some things will not stand the test of time and will be abolished, but sometimes things do remain. And this is also true when a sovereign power is conquered by another sovereign power and occupied for generations. Eventually, that conquering sovereign power may leave, but they may have had a permanent impact on the setting that they had formerly occupied.

With all that said, we're going to talk about different government types. And these can be organized in different ways, such as by the power structure or the power source. And the latter is what we are going to use here. So, the first thing we're going to talk about is authoritative states.

AUTHORITATIVE STATES

The first authoritative state we're going to talk about is the autocracy. This basically means one person is in charge and they can do whatever they want without any consequence. This is the sort of leader who can kill someone in broad daylight rather than having their guys go and kidnap someone and do it in a back alley somewhere. We tend to really like this idea for fantasy and science fiction villains who are running a country because this gives our hero someone to destroy.

We don't need good reasons for this person being so evil because we can always fall back on that idea that absolute power corrupts absolutely. We may not want to say that because it's a cliche, but the idea holds true. We can give this person any reason to be the way they are. It could be their ego, it could be their personality in some other way, or it could be the fact that they have witnessed that sort of abuse by their predecessors. It could also be fear of someone taking over and doing the same things to them.

We'll be discussing these more in a few minutes, but absolute monarchies, like Brunei and Saudi Arabia, and dictatorships are the main forms of autocracy. There's almost not that much to explain to this because it's relatively simple in that one person has so much unchecked power.

The simplicity of this also makes it somewhat appealing to us if we haven't taken the time to research more complicated forms of government. This could even be expected in the genres, and that might be one reason to avoid it in favor of something that takes a little bit more research and skill to depict.

The next authoritative state we'll talk about is the totalitarian government. In a totalitarian government, the state has total control of everything, which is, of course, why it's called that. This means military, communications and even the infrastructure, like your water source and your electricity. There's only one political party and they use a lot of propaganda to remain in power and control the minds of the citizens who have no power at all. And there's not going to be any law to protect people or get them what they want from their lives.

You have few, if any rights. If you try to speak your mind in this sort of regime, the punishment could be really brutal. We're talking about not only death, but mass killings and long prison sentences, or even hard labor. The military is also used to enforce the will of whoever is in charge. And this can also mean that there is a cult of personality where everyone is supposed to worship this person. This is the sort of government that has a secret police, and they use the state to terrorize people into submission. If you're looking to create the good versus evil sort of dynamic, this is the sort of government that many of us would consider evil.

If you live somewhere that has this government type, or if you are visiting, it's going to have a major impact on your stories. So, you should have a pretty good understanding of what life might be like there in order to set your story there. And if you don't want your story to be that impacted by the government, then you probably should not choose this. Maybe you should choose some-thing a little bit more generic, like a monarchy.

One of the ways that this government type arises is af-ter a war when there has been a lot of destruction, and the existing government type might have been destroyed dur-ing that war, such as many of the people leading a democ-racy being killed or the political party being destroyed in some way, or just upset enough that a balance of power shifts too much in one direction and one political party seizes all control. So, if you're trying to figure out how such a regime can come to be, this is one option.

A totalitarian government can also form after anarchy when there is no government at all. What these scenarios have in common is a power vacuum that is filled by some-one with a lot of political allies. This is part of why in the United States the founders created different branches of government to try to prevent anyone from getting that much power, or even one political party gaining that much power. That sort of power leads to abuse.

Now, if we like the idea of a totalitarian government, but we find it a little bit too extreme, we can go with an-other type which is known as an authoritarian govern-ment. Power here is not so absolute and all-encompassing. There will still be one political power, and that could ei-ther be an individual or a group. But one of the differences between an authoritarian government and a totalitarian one is that the latter has a cult of personality designed to worship the leader, who is usually very charismatic. But in an authoritarian one, the guy may actually be disliked. One of the reasons this still works is that he is not in as much control of the government.

Another difference is that in an authoritarian govern-ment, the state is mostly concerned with aspects of politi-cal life, not everything else. So, it's possible for someone to do things like own a business and have a certain amount of rights, or at least the illusion of control. However, that control is mostly over their own lives, not the political establishment. That is being tightly controlled by those who are in power. There will be a legislature in this kind of government, but there is so much corruption and red tape that, basically, those who are in charge can stall any progress on something that they disagree with and they don't want to see it go forward.

This is, again, part of the illusion of what life is really like there where they allow people to think that they have more freedom than they do. Someone may be able to introduce a bill that would change the way the state works, but the state would basically kill it. In a totalitarian one, you wouldn't even be allowed to do that, and if you said anything about it, you'd be killed. Some examples of an authoritarian government include Laos, Egypt, China, Vietnam and North Korea.

The last authoritative state we're going to talk about is the famous one: dictatorships. When one person or party rules a country, that's a dictatorship. And that does bear some resemblance to some of what we were just talking about. But one of the things to keep in mind here is that this is almost a role in government more than a type of one. One basic reason for this is that it's basically impossible for one person to rule everyone. They're going to need a whole bunch of people to support them. And sometimes that leader is nothing more than a figurehead of a party or a small, elite group of people who are actually in charge. And this person is the public face of that dictatorship.

So, that begs the question, "What type of government is it really?" And the answer is it's either authoritarian or it's totalitarian. So, to reiterate, a dictatorship is not a type of government, it's more of a role in an authoritarian or a totalitarian government. This means when you are creating a dictatorship and you're calling it that in your notes, for example, you should still figure out which type of government it really has, and the answer is not "dictatorship." When we say it's a dictatorship, we're really talking about the authoritarian or totalitarian governments that are run by a dictator and his inner circle, and that's why we're calling it a dictatorship.

On the other hand, if we want to be vague and not make a decision about what the government type really is, then a dictatorship is a good way to imply a certain level of brutality. One reason we may want to do that is so that we can make up our minds later. Like some of the other brutal regimes, a dictatorship can arise when there is a government that has collapsed and either a leader or a military group exerts control. Sometimes it is actually elected presidents or prime ministers who seize power by crushing the opposition and then creating a one-party rule. All we really need is a power vacuum and someone to seize control.

One last note on dictatorships is that a new dictator may want to prove to any surrounding sovereign powers that they are a force to be reckoned with and, as a result, they stage a series of attacks. On the other hand, if the dictator has been around for 20 or 30 years and has already established himself, then he may not want to upset the balance of power in the region. And it's not because he's trying to be nice. It's more because he's protecting his own status quo. After all, what if he attacks someone and he loses, and then attacks someone else and he loses? Then he starts to lose stature and be seen weak by his own people. And, as a result, he may be taken over by somebody else.

Part of what we're getting at is that dictators can act differently from each other, it's going to depend on how long this dictatorship has lasted. Keep this in mind when creating one. Finally, some examples of this are the Soviet Union under Joseph Stalin and, of course, Nazi Germany.

DEMOCRACY

Let's talk about democracies. One of the basic ideas of democracy is that people are allowed to participate in government and they have influence over what becomes a law. Now, you may not have heard of this, but there are two versions of this. One of them is called direct democracy, and the other one is indirect democracy. The direct kind means that people vote directly on the initiative that is supposed to become law. The indirect kind means that we actually appoint people, such as senators and congressmen, and they do the voting for us. Many of you will recognize this because that's basically the way the United States is set up. However, it is possible in the United States for people to vote directly on some initiatives. Many of those direct initiatives are voted on at the state level, or even at smaller levels like the county.

With the indirect kind, we are voting for people to do our biding, and if we don't like the way they have done things, we end up voting them out of office. This gives rise to a scenario where a politician tells us what we want to hear in order to get elected, and then they don't necessarily follow through and then they end up losing the next election. Because we can vote people in and out of office, this has eliminated the need for something like a revolution. We can create change in a more peaceful way. And government is supposed to reflect the will of the people, not some all-powerful leader.

Democracy as a concept, and even a reality, has existed for thousands of years, but it's really only been in the last couple hundred years that it's become one of the major forms of government. Before that, there tended to be a small group of people known as an oligarchy who were running a country. Now, just because we create a democracy, that does not mean that our characters who are experiencing that form of government, whether they live there or they're traveling through it – it doesn't mean that they're not going to run into problems.

For example, even though equal rights are supposed to be one of the things that happens in a democracy, we all know that there is bias, whether it's gender bias or racism. There can also be bias against immigrants, whether they are legal or illegal. If there's a lack of freedom in someone's home country, that could be the reason they have journeyed to the country where the story is taking place, like the United States if it was happening here on Earth. As we all know, the United States has been looked up to as a place where people can come to for greater freedom in their lives. But, of course, so many people have done so that we have a pretty strict immigration policy, as do a lot of other countries that have a better standard of living.

When we are creating sovereign powers, we probably want to create multiple types in a sense that some of them have a good standard of living, like a democracy, and some of them have a terrible one like in the dictatorship. One sovereign power will be a place to avoid and another one will be a place that is sought after. This is a truly great reason to have a better understanding of government types and use them for variety. Characters will be well known for having originated from one place or another. There's a tendency in fantasy and sci-fi to just say that someone is from so-and-so country and not only not mention what kind of government type it has, but – and we don't necessarily want to get into explaining that to people, but another character should have an opinion of what life must have been like for that character.

If they're from the Kingdom of Kysh, and that's an absolute monarchy where people have almost no rights, then someone should say, "I can see why you left," or something to that effect. Or they might just assume that this person's relatives are living in a harsh world, or maybe they've even been killed. On the other hand, if I'm the person from a dictatorship and I found out that you're from a country like the United States, I might assume that your life has been really great, and maybe I'm jealous.

Now, when it comes to the rise and fall of democracy, usually something must change in order for this significant level of change to occur. This is true of any government type. They don't just suddenly end for no reason. If there has been a dictator, for example, who has been abusing power, and this person is killed in some way, or just dethroned, then the people could have been fed up for so long that they go ahead and try to create a democracy. If that sounds too simple and farfetched, well, that's exactly what happened when the United States formed and threw off England as its ruler.

But a democracy can also fall when things become too heavily sided in one direction or another. Right now in the United States, one political party has more power than the other. And if that continued to go in that direction, and the people in that party were willing to give up democracy, then we could actually move away from a democracy towards a more authoritarian government. This could not only happen from things becoming too one-sided, but it's possible that the government wasn't setup with enough checks on balances of power. If there weren't enough laws to stop a leader from doing something, then maybe you could get away with it.

In extremely recent times, such as this year in the United States, in 2018, we actually have a president and a political party who don't seem to care as much about threatening this balance of power. And people have even talked about supreme court nominees potentially pushing things even further in one direction. And some people are rightly worried that this could ultimately lead to a destruction of democracy to at least some degree.

There are some additional details in the *Creating Places* book, but I'm not going to cover those today.

FEDERATIONS

Let's talk about federations. As it turns out, there's more than one type of federation, but one of them is actually called federation. The others are a unitary state, the confederation, and, of course, the empire. Let's first cover the federation.

This is a union of self-governing states or regions that give up some of their freedom for a national government and some other advantages. There is a constitution and it outlines the status and the division of power, and this cannot be altered by political powers, the federal government, or any of the regions in the union.

One goal of that union is greater stability, which can be economic. One of the problems with that is that if one of the states has a serious economic problem, it can actually affect all of them. Suddenly, what seems like a good idea might not seem like a good idea anymore to all those who are affected. Another reason for joining a federation is that if there are territorial disputes, this will also be resolved with the agreement. In other words, a federation can put an end to war. Now, we may not like this idea because it could interfere with our setting if we are trying to have countries who are at war, or characters who are being affected by war.

In an earlier episode, we talked about the concept of sovereignty, which is basically whether or not you are self-governing. And when it comes to a federation, the individual states are self-governing, but they don't have any power at the federal level or with any foreign power. And all states in the federation may not be equal because some of them may have joined before newer laws came into play and impacted later powers that joined. Of course, that sort of imbalance of power can also lead to problems.

The central government is tasked with trying to find a solution that will satisfy all the states in the federation, so this can be a big task. If we have a character who is in that federal government, they might have a lot of problems on their hands. However, this is not normally the sort of thing that people find interesting, so we're going to have to make this really be character-based and impactful in the story in such a way that it makes it interesting to our readers.

If they fail to resolve these conflicts, this could lead to civil war. And there's a really good example of this. It's called the United States Civil War. I'm going to simplify the issue, but basically the southern states in the United States thought that the constitution gave them the right for slavery, and the other states disagreed with this. Now, slavery was a basic part of the economy in the south, which felt like it wasn't going to survive very well without it. And, as a result, war broke out. The southern states tried to create the Confederation, which is another form of federation that we'll talk about in a minute. But one of the problems that the south faced is that no foreign country would recognize that the south had sovereignty over itself. So, this was going to be a problem. The federal government in D.C. fought the war partly to bring the southern states back in line.

A final note on federations is the naming convention. Sometimes they actually do have the word "federation" in their title, but a place like Canada does not. And there are other titles that can be used, such as a confederation, a federal republic, dominion, kingdom and even union. The only real problem for us as world builders with these titles is that we can't always tell what form of government something is just by the word that we have put on it.

Let's talk about the unitary state. This is very similar to a federation except that the federal government can completely eliminate the autonomy of the states. The way this forms is also a little bit different because a federation comes together when independent states join forces, but a unitary state originates from a preexisting central government granting more autonomy to those previously dependent states. For example, imagine that a country like the United States suddenly set free, so to speak, the 50 states making it up, and became a unitary state where those states now have more autonomy over themselves. But one of the things about a unitary state is that just as it can give that autonomy to the states, it can also take it back. The unitary state's central government can literally abolish a state altogether at will.

This is an interesting scenario where a state could be existing for a long time, but maybe it's doing things that the central government's leader doesn't like. And so, he simply abolishes the state altogether. The United Kingdom is an example of a unitary state.

Let's talk more about a confederation, which I mentioned a few minutes ago. This is when a group of sovereign powers forms a permanent union so they can act together against other states. And membership is voluntary, which is very different from a federation. A state that's part of a confederation can simply leave if they so choose. We once again may find this to be a little bit less interesting because we kind of like it when someone is being constrained by something, they try to do it anyway, that causes a problem because somebody like another government or part of their own government goes after them and we have this conflict. If you can simply take your ball and walk away or go home, there's less drama to that.

A confederation usually forms by a treaty, but the agreements are not binding until the member states create laws that are in accordance with those agreements. Some examples of a confederation are Switzerland, Canada, Belgium and the European Union.

EMPIRES

The last one we want to talk about is the empire. This is a little bit different from everything we've been talking about because in this case we have multiple sovereign powers who are being ruled by a single power. For example, the Roman Empire conquered one sovereign power after another and absorbed all of them into its own Roman Empire. By contrast, France was only a kingdom when Napoleon decided it was an empire, even though they did not yet rule other sovereign powers. And he did this partly so that he could declare himself emperor. After all, why be a king when you can be an emperor? The British Empire included territories that were far across the sea. So, this is another option for us.

Empires always form as a result of coercion, which can be a war where you defeat the other sovereign power, or it can be something like economics. Sometimes a weak state is simply annexed by an empire for protection and other advantages such as trade, and they might be perfectly okay with this. It's always better for even an empire to not go to war, so if they can coerce, in some other fashion, another sovereign power to join the empire, they will do so.

One of the problems that an empire faces is simply the physical size of it. And it's not going to have troops to maintain control over all of that. So, having a certain amount of peaceful interaction with the sovereign powers that it has absorbed is going to go a long way to making it stable. Another issue you can face is having, basically, racism going on where different ethnic groups that were part of different sovereign powers have now both been absorbed by one empire, and now they have to act like they get along. This may work for a time, but there could be simmering hatred. And if the empire ever falls, then those ethnic groups and their respective sovereign powers may go right back to fighting with each other.

It should also be noted that if you are being ruled by an empire, and you're in a previously independent sovereign power, and then the empire falls and your sovereign power is suddenly freed, well, that's no longer going to have its own government. Actually, that may not be true. It might have a government, but the point really is that there's still a sudden change to the government, so this is another opportunity to suddenly change the type of government that we have in one of our sovereign powers.

So, if an empire falls, we could have one sovereign power that becomes a dictatorship, another one that becomes a constitutional monarchy, and another one that becomes a democracy. Generally, if an empire collapses, this is often catastrophic for any of the sovereign powers that it was ruling over.

MONARCHIES

Time to talk about everyone's favorite, the monarchy, which is what a kingdom is technically called. This used to be the most common form of government until the republic eventually took over. So, if you're writing fantasy and you keep using this, well, maybe there's a reason for that. A federation is arguably more common in science fiction.

In a monarchy, the person in charge, the monarch, is sovereign until death or abdication. As we all know, a monarchy is typically hereditary, with only the members of the family, such as the males, becoming a monarch. If we would like to be more progressive, we can have women also have this ability. The heirs are raised in a royal family and taught what is expected of them. And if the same family rules for many generations, that is called a dynasty.

Now, sometimes the path of succession, who becomes the next monarch, is not always clear. And that actually lead to the War of the Roses, which, in turn, inspired George R.R. Martin's *Game of Thrones*. Some of the succession stuff is a little bit confusing, so I don't want to go into the details here in the podcast, but the details are found on the website and, of course, in *Creating Places*.

What I want to talk about instead is the difference between an absolute and constitutional monarchy. I briefly talked about the absolute monarchy earlier when I mentioned the authoritative states. An absolute monarch is one who is above the law and can get away with anything. Precisely because such persons abused their power, there were resistances that slowly built up in one kingdom, and then in another. And, over time, a new form developed and that's called a constitutional monarchy. What's happened in this case is that the monarch has become the head of state, which I explained in the last episode, and then there is a parliament with a prime minister, and that prime minister is the one who is the head of government.

What we're talking about here is that all of this power that one person had has been disseminated to other people. One result is less abuse of power. The constitution is actually what exists to place those limits on the monarchy. Now, you may be wondering, as I often did, what can people get away with? What can a monarch do and what can the prime minister do? And the answer is that it really depends on the country, and the result is that we can do whatever we want when we are inventing a sovereign power that has a constitutional monarchy. This is one area where we don't need to feel like we have to get it right because we can make it up.

OLIGARCHIES

Now, there is one last group of government types known as oligarchies. What they have in common is that a group of people is in charge. Anything can really be the basis for an oligarchy, such as a group that has unusual wealth or military power, status, family, higher education or even an ability like with wizards. An aristocracy is a form of government where a privileged class of people is supposedly the most qualified and, therefore, they are in charge. In a plutocracy, it's a small group of rich people. In a military junta, as you would expect, the military is in charge and the government type is usually authoritative. Then there's a timocracy, where only property owners can participate in government. And then there's a theocracy, where a religious person or group is in charge. Although, the reason they are in charge is that they are supposedly given that position by a god, who is the ultimate authority.

Now, if you've ever wondered what a nation is, or a country, I do go into some detail in *Creating Places* about what these are and what these words really mean, and it might surprise you. They are not government types, however. I'm also not going to go into detail on how to choose a form of government or how to create the history, although I did mention a little bit of this. And another subject that I cover in the book is how many different powers you should invent.

In our next episode, we're going to continue discussing the subject of creating sovereign powers.

HOW TO CREATE
SOVEREIGN POWERS

Hello and welcome to *The Art of World Building Podcast*, episode number fourteen, part 3. Today's topic is how population, location, climate, symbols, and tensions between a sovereign power and others can all enrich your kingdom, republic, dictatorship, and more. Why have them all be the same when little details can bring out the vividness? This material and more is discussed in chapter 5 of *Creating Places*, volume 2 in *The Art of World Building* book series.

THE POPULATION

The first thing I want to talk about is the population of our sovereign power. After all, the people and our characters are the whole point. Something that's fairly obvious once it's been pointed out is that we should consider which species are likely to live there based on the land features that are available. For example, in fantasy, dwarves are typically living either in mountains or rolling hills. If our sovereign power is located almost exclusively on a grassland, then there probably aren't going to be too many dwarves who call this their home. The same would be true of elves if we accept the idea that they prefer the forests.

On the other hand, if the sovereign power includes a territory that does have a forest or a mountain range or rolling hills, then the species that live in those are going to be more concentrated in that area. All of this is something to keep in mind when we are laying out a sovereign power. The great thing about it is that it's a built in way of deciding where people are. The work is virtually done for us by the geography. All we need to say in our files of information or in our stories is that there is a certain type of terrain in a given area and, therefore, the dwarves, the elves or whoever are more commonly found in that area.

Let's take a specific example of this. Let's say that on the eastern side of this sovereign power that is mostly a plain, a grassland, there is a forest. But then, farther to the west, several hundred miles away, there is another, much larger forest where there are also elves. We might have a human character encounter an elf and wonder out loud, or even just in their own mind, "Okay, which forest is this guy from? Is he someone from my own sovereign power, or is he someone from that other forest that is several hundred miles away?"

One way he might be able to tell is if elves are accepted as a member of the sovereign power, then the elf might be wearing a symbol that identifies him as belonging to this sovereign power, especially if those other elves that are farther away are considered enemies. After all, he wouldn't want to be mistaken for one. Then again, those elves that are farther away, and who are enemies, might purposefully figure out how to wear clothing that looks like this, and then infiltrate this sovereign power doing this, by pretending they are the elves that are from that area.

This is a pretty simple and effective way to give an impression of more dynamics to our setting. It also makes it easier to not have everywhere be just the same and some sort of generic place. When we are laying out a sovereign power, we might want to purposely include parts of different land features inside the borders of that sovereign power. Of course, one issue that could result is that there might be a forest that the elves believe belongs to them, but then part of that forest is seen as part of one sovereign power, and then another part of it is seen as belonging to yet another sovereign power, so that we sort of have three different groups who are claiming areas of this land.

Hopefully you remember from the previous episodes that if more than one sovereign power is claiming they are sovereign over a territory, that means that neither of them really are until one of them falls. So, all we really need to do here is decide that a land feature has a given species living in it and that another sovereign power has claimed some of that area as its own. If this other sovereign power has completely taken over or surrounded that land feature, then maybe those living in it consider themselves part of that sovereign power. But, either way, there could certainly still be some hostility going on here.

Another issue to bear in mind is that monster or other undesirable animals could be inside that land feature. As a result, even though that area has supposedly been conquered, there are things in there that are a problem for the people who are living in that general area. This is, once again, something that we can make use of because people from a given area of the sovereign power might be living near a dangerous land feature. Not because of the feature itself, necessarily, like a volcano that might erupt, but because of the things that live in that land feature, or are on it. Just as we consider one area of our own country to have a certain kind of weather or reputation, maybe that area of the sovereign power that is dangerous has a reputation because of what's there.

Part of what I'm getting at with all of this is that we don't really want a sovereign power that is just uniform across its entire territory. There should be areas that are seen as being one way versus another, and that there is contrast. This keeps things more interesting, and also realistic. Right now, we're talking about population and type, but we can also do that with the weather. In other episodes, we talked about how climate can be different on one side of a continent versus the other because of things like prevailing winds. And this is something that we should make use of to create more variety. Now, when it comes to these undesirable creatures or monsters, our sovereign power could have specialized fighting forces who are experts at dealing with this. Naturally, these people might be trained and stationed in the area where they are going to encounter this problem.

We can also decide that this country is known for having people who are good at fighting this threat. Maybe there's a training center there and maybe people from other sovereign powers that are friendly to this one come here for training and experience dealing with it. This can help give our characters some backstory. If we have a knight from one sovereign power, he could have spent time in another sovereign power gaining a certain kind of experience, and now it is years later and he is off on our story and he has a certain amount of world experience as a result of this. We could have him encounter a citizen from that sovereign power where they trained him, and he knows cultural things or even language issues and is able to relate to that person and say, "Oh, yeah. You know, I spent two years training at this city and this region where you've got these monsters," or whatever. This is a great and be-lievable way to add some diversity to our character and make it seem like people did not just grow up in a little fish bowl where they have no outside experience.

Maybe this knight even has a certain amount of reputa-tion because he trained with those people, especially of those people have a reputation for being good at fighting this problem. People can look at our knight character and say, "Well, you must be really good at it, too. Maybe you can help us with the same creature here," or, "We've got a similar one and you would be the most qualified. There-fore, we're going to ask for your help in dealing with this."

So, lack of uniformity in our sovereign power is a good thing. There's a tendency among us human authors to cre-ate sovereign powers that were created by humans for humans, and where any other species that we have invent-ed are just bit players on that stage. This might be some-thing that we want to challenge. And in science fiction, that probably does get challenged a little bit more than in fantasy. I'm speculating, but the reason for this is likely the prevalence of aliens from different planets merging on some sort of moon or whatever. You know, there are these stations where people get together. There's just all this interconnectivity that is assumed to be taking place. By contrast, we almost have more racism built in where eve-ryone is holed up in their area and not wanting much to do with everybody else.

The elves are too snobby, or whatever. They're elitists. I forget what the usual stereotype is for dwarves, but they basically stay underground. So, everyone's got some sort of prejudice that keeps them there. The question is whether we want to continue doing this trope, or do we want to expand and do something new? Either way, we should de-cide who is in power in this sovereign power and what percentage of each population is. We probably don't want to go with hard numbers because that's not really going to translate for most people, and it also kind of binds us. It's a little more flexible to just go with a percentage, like saying the dwarves are about 20% of the population, the elves are 15%, and maybe the humans are 54% and the rest is a hodgepodge of other things. I wasn't paying attention to my math there, so hopefully I didn't go over 100%, but you get the idea.

Something else to bear in mind is that whatever species created that settlement, they may not be the only ones who are in power anymore. This is going to depend on the age of the sovereign power or the settlements within that sovereign power. You may remember from the previous episodes that a given form of a sovereign power, its type of government, does not last forever. They come and go. It could be a kingdom one century and it could be a dictatorship for 20 years. It could then be a totalitarian government for another 30 years and then switch back to something like a constitutional monarchy, and then, later, it's going to be a republic. So, this changes a lot. And each time the form of government changes, it's possible that new species are more prevalent in this sovereign power.

The practical impact is that 200, or even 1,000 years ago, let's say the elves were a small percentage of the population. But now it's 2,000 years later and they're a much larger percentage. When this newest form of government forms, maybe they are an inherent part of it and so are aspects of their culture. To me, this is a much more believable scenario, assuming that there is territory of this sovereign power that includes the typical elven homeland in this case. You know, the terrain of forests.

Now, we could be thinking that each time a sovereign power collapses, its territory gets divided up into smaller bits. And that can happen, but a new sovereign power can essentially take the place of the old one and have more or less the same territory. It might shrink a little bit, it might grow in one direction or another – literally one compass point or another – but it's going to cover much of the same territory. The fact that a new government has taken over, and maybe renamed the country, doesn't mean that the sovereign power as a whole has really vanished. It's just kind of reinvented itself. In order for it to really vanish, you would have to bomb it off the face of the earth so that no one lives in that entire territory anymore.

So, it's still going to be there. The people that made up the previous incarnation of this sovereign power will still make up the new incarnation of this sovereign power. If we've got a mix of species, like elves, dwarves and humans, and some sort of outside force conquered this sovereign power, but then didn't have the armed forces to maintain control over it and left, those species that were there before are still there, and they're going to need a new form of government. When they form that, they may still do so together. They're not necessarily going to be just the humans forming it, and the others have no say. If they've been around for a while, then maybe they've changed their minds about how they want to do things and are inclusive.

You know, this does happen. People don't necessarily just shove people out. What I'm talking about there, by shoving people out, is excluding them from the new government. If it's going to be a more authoritative state, then maybe they do. But if it's going to be a new form of democracy or a federal republic, then those are more inclusive by nature. And this is how we're going to end up with laws that say, "Yes, the elves can be elected prime minister," for example. And if you're thinking it's only elves who are going to be pushing for that, that's not necessarily true. In the United States, the founders tried to make things inclusive from the very beginning. This has mostly lasted since then, although it has had problems and challenges. But the basic vision of inclusion was created by white men where they wanted to give more rights to others.

Now, some of that wasn't there in the beginning. Eventually, women had to be given more rights, like voting rights, and others had to be given more rights. But the basic idea of the country being inclusive was there from its founding. So, even though white men arguably founded the country, or were involved in creating the documents like the Declaration of Independence and the Constitution, today, we've had a black president and it's been a long fight to get to that point. But this is the kind of thing that we can do in our sovereign powers that we are inventing.

What I'm getting at here is that we should decide who invented the sovereign power a long time ago, and then how things have changed as time has progressed, and who was involved in the new formation of the sovereign power, and what kind of rights do they have? In order to do that, we need to understand our population. And, in order to do that, we should have an idea of what land features are included in our sovereign power's territory.

RELATIONS WITH OTHER SOVEREIGN POWERS

Since we've been talking about relationships within a sovereign power, let's talk about that a little bit more and how that can be affected by relationships with other sovereign powers. All good stories need tension, and even in the gaming world, we need to have reason for our characters to go from one place to another. So, let's talk about causes of tension.

The first up is going to be ethnicity. This is similar to racism and is an unfortunate reality that we can use in our work. If we'd prefer not to include this in our work, then it's better to not comment on it at all and just ignore it than to actually comment on it and say that there is no ethnic hatred because that's not really realistic. It's a nice end state that maybe humanity or other species of our invention will one day get to, but we're not there and I doubt it's going to happen any time, even on fictional worlds. But if you don't want to do anything with ethnic hatred, then just ignore the subject rather than saying, "Everyone gets along fine," because that's not realistic. It's also not interesting.

In general, with ethnic hatred, what happens is that unfavorable attributes, such as character, are assigned to a group of people who usually share physical traits, and that makes them easier to physically identify on sight. Usually, we're talking about facial features like the shape and size of the nose, or the eyebrows, the jaw, even the mouth. Really anything. In a world with fictional species, we can use other features that are more prominent, like the pointed ears of elves or a lot of the brow ridges that you see on characters in something like *Star Trek.*

If you want to create ethnic hatred, one of the things that you can do is just decide that people in a given region of your world have certain physical features. There doesn't need to be any rhyme or reason for those. It's just going to be the way it is. What I mean is that those features are not going to have anything to do with where they live. It's just that people who have those features have congregated in that area for a certain amount of time, and now they are associated with that area and they are an actual ethnic group. People typically just assign negative character traits to a group of people with whom they have experienced tension before. It might have been some sort of dispute, and it could have been anything from cultural to ideological, or something based on the form of government.

We almost don't need to do a deep dive into this. We could decide that one culture is really big on personal freedom, and another one is not. And, as a result, they really have a problem with the way those manifest in each other. And, as a result, they have associated that form of government with bad behavior, for example, in their opinion, and associated that with the physical features. So, therefore, it becomes not just a general hatred, but a hatred that is associated with the ethnicity of the people who exhibit those physical traits and those behaviors.

As usual, we can take analogues from Earth, whether that's an actual ethnic issue from Earth or something cultural that we've decided to assign to one ethnic group versus another. For example, abortion rights and even gun rights are hot issues. So is homosexuality and whether this is accepted. All we really need to do is assign one side of this argument to one group, and the other side to the other group, and associate this with ethnicity because of physical features and have it be a more localized issue. That's how that comes about. You know, in our modern world, we're also interconnected, so these are not issues that have anything to do with ethnic groups. It's a more widespread issue than that. But we can do the same thing on a more local region, and that's how it becomes an ethnic issue.

This brings up another source of tension that can happen with a sovereign power, or between one and another. And that is the worldview. We can use countries on Earth, again, as examples. For example, we have some that are known for being democracies and others that are known for being these authoritative regimes that are really brutal to people. Something that can happen is that countries can end up fighting proxy wars. For example, the United States likes to see democracy spread. So, sometimes we assist other countries in becoming a democracy.

By contrast, communist countries have typically supported each other for the same reason. At times, we've had the United States propping up one country, and another country, like Russia, propping up a different one and turning this into a kind of proxy war where the United States and Russia are not going at each other directly. They are fighting each other ideologically through countries that each one of them is supporting.

Another source of conflict is resources. Earlier, I talked to you about having a forest that is partially or completely inside a given sovereign power. Well, what if there's something in that forest, whether it's the trees or something special that we've invented, and it's rare and, therefore, the sovereign power has total control of it, or at least partial control of it, and somebody else wants that thing? Well, now we've got a source of conflict. This is another thing to bear in mind when you are laying out where your sovereign power's borders are.

On that note, territory is another source of conflict. Aside from the obvious reason we were just discussing, it could be an issue where something like a landlocked sovereign power wants access to the sea and it can't get to it unless it conquers another territory. Of course, if both sovereign powers in question are democracies, then maybe they work together in a more peaceful way. But if one of them is totalitarian, like a dictatorship, and the democracy is the one that has the access to the sea, it's probable that the totalitarian government is going to attack instead of negotiate. Unless it's going to do something like build up its nuclear weapons, for example, using an example on Earth, and say, "Hey, we're only going to give up these weapons if you give us access to the sea."

This goes on in the real world where sometimes countries build up an arsenal not because they're intending to use it, but as a bargaining chip. It's always smart to go into negotiations with something to trade.

IDENTIFYING SOVEREIGN POWERS

Let's take up one of the easier subjects in world building, and that is the different ways that we can identify our sovereign powers. Sometimes it feels like there's a lot of research or other things we need to do and spend a lot of time on something, but this is one area of world building that we can just do one at a time or in batches and just kind of quickly get this done and move on. It's relatively lightweight. What we're talking about here are symbols, flags and slogans like you see in *Game of Thrones*. These are used to identify a sovereign power. Of course, they can also be used to identify smaller units like a settlement.

On one hand, this is a minor subject, but the symbols are important exactly because they are symbols. We can create a brooding, intimidating symbol for an authoritarian power, and then something that's a little more welcoming for a democracy. These symbols will be emblazoned on things like ships or battle stations or the walls of a castle or just the flag that's flying overhead. They can also be incorporated into the uniforms that characters are wearing. Along with the colors, these symbols are a good way of quickly getting across an impression. This is one of our great uses for them as storytellers.

That said, I do think this is something that should be invented later in your development of a sovereign power because you're going to want to understand what your sovereign power is like and what it may represent to other people before going too far with something like this. However, you can always change your mind. If you decide that your symbol is really cool but maybe it doesn't go with the sovereign power you originally associated it with, you can just take it off and put it on another one, provided you haven't actually published something using that.

The goal of any identifier we choose is to not only identify that power, but to embody or portray a fundamental trait of that power. And they can inspire fear, loathing, love, indifference, or they can also be a rallying cry during a war. And when our characters are traveling and they are going to arrive somewhere, they're going to be on the lookout for these symbols. And failure to mention them is a bit of an oversight. Imagine, even on Earth, if you were on a boat in the ocean and a ship was approaching you, and it was a military one, would you be looking to see what country it belonged to? Because if it's from Russia or the United States, that could have a very different impact on what's going to happen to you.

When it comes to symbols, these may change each time the sovereign power itself changes. In fact, this is more likely than not because the new government wants a literal symbol of the fact that it is a new government and it's not the previous one. There's been a change. Of course, they could also change the name of the country, for example, but it's still going to want a symbol. But it doesn't have to change, especially if the symbol is something that is very cherished to the people. Also, if the symbol is a geographic feature like a mountain that's distinctive, then that's probably not going to change if that mountain is still within the territory of the sovereign power.

That brings up an interesting scenario of that land feature being in a territory that has been conquered by another sovereign power, and now the symbol of this sovereign power is located in another sovereign power. That's probably going to be a big point of pride and something that really bothers people. Bear in mind that an authoritative government is going to have a more intimidating and bold symbol, and even the colors, to imply the impression and dominance of that government power. Even the architecture in such a sovereign power can reflect the attitude of the people who are in control. On the other hand, a democracy might want softer colors and a less threatening and more inclusive symbol.

We should be sure to make a comment about the impression that any symbol we invent makes. If we just say that it's a hawk, that doesn't really tell us what it looks like. It could be depicted in a benign position, or one where it's kind of attacking, or one where it looks majestic. These differences are pretty important. When it comes to color, a domineering government is going to choose a primary color such as red. They can also use things like black and white because these are fairly stark. Colors certainly come into play when it comes to flags because many of the simplest flags here on Earth are simply a horizontal stripe of one or more colors.

These colors don't have to signify anything to us, but it's always better if they do. Although, the average person often forgets what the colors may mean. I think that this is an area of world building we can usually skip because the average person reading our work is not going to care what the colors mean. What they care about is the impression. Bear in mind that the flags should be relatively easy to depict. Because, in our modern world, we have machines that can create really elaborate designs, but you may have noticed that most flags are not that involved. That's probably because they're very old when it was relatively easy to sow together two or three different horizontal stripes that are each in a different color in order to make a flag.

So, if we're doing fantasy where the technology is not like our modern world, we might want to go with pretty simple flags. But if we're doing science fiction where technology is far in excess of what we have here, then we may want to go with something that's a little bit more elaborate. The more advanced it is, the harder it is for the average person to depict that flag.

THE IMPACT OF LOCATION

I want to say a few words about the location of our sovereign power because, as the old adage goes, location is everything. We've already talked about how land features can influence this, but I want to go into this a little bit more. The example that I'm going to use first is that if we have an island nation, then this can really impact the culture that originates in that place because they are going to be relying on the sea not only for transportation, but for things like fish. As a result, they might be not only very good at sailing, but they might be explorers.

On one hand, this is so obvious that it almost seems like a cliché, but it's also so obvious that it would not make sense to not do this. However, if that nation is relatively young, it may not have the industry to really build ships to do that. And, as a result, it might be the kind of place that is easily conquered by others who do have that industry and the resulting skill at sailing. They also might not be good at fighting, so that they get conquered even though they are good at sailing. So, on one hand, the fact that they might do a lot of sailing could suggest that they are a seafaring power and that they're someone to be feared on the seas, but it doesn't necessarily have to be. They could also be a victim.

Something else we can also leverage is the proximity to the equator. Here on Earth, we still need to use the equator to help us lift off into space. The reason is that it's easier to get to that kind of altitude if we are closer to the equator because the Earth spins faster there. In science fiction, we could decide that the engines are so powerful that this is no longer a concern, or we could decide that the world that we're creating is a little bit more like our modern one where they still need to use certain kinds of rockets that benefit from being close to the equator. One scenario that can be helpful here is that if a sovereign power wants to launch something into space, but it's not near enough to the equator, then it's probably going to want to form alliances with a sovereign power that does have that territory.

I hope one thing that you're picking up from all of this is the way we can create allegiances and enemies with sovereign powers based on terrain and location. We can also decide to use the landscape as a way of characterizing the sovereign power itself, and even justifying the forms of government that have been found there. It's a bit simplistic, and almost a cliché, to say that a foreboding and intimidating landscape, like a desert, is therefore going to give rise to a totalitarian or authoritative government, but the idea does have some appeal. The idea is that the landscape is harsh and, therefore, so are the people. On the other hand, if it's more like a paradise, then maybe everyone is kind of soft and the government is benevolent.

The climate might also affect this. For example, if the sovereign power is centered right over the equator, then it's going to be pretty hot and rainy. Therefore, people are not going to be wearing heavy, long clothes. As a result, something like a man wearing a full suit of plate armor might be relatively uncommon and just not part of what they do there because that's hot, it's heavy and it's not something you're really going to wear in that climate. This is not to say that it can't be done, but that is something that originated on Earth in colder climates. Actually, that may not be true. I haven't really looked into that, but it does seem plausible.

We should also pay attention to how easy it is to access this sovereign power. If it's very mountainous, then maybe people have a hard time getting there. This could also inhibit people from successfully attacking it in war unless they are doing so from the air. These are things to keep in mind because you might expect the military in such a place to not focus so much on ground forces, but on aerial forces for defense. As I mentioned earlier, it's likely that there's more than one terrain in this power. So, different areas of it are going to be impacted in different ways. This means that those who are really good at flying on great birds of prey might be doing so in one area of the region, and found frequently there, but on another area, where it's mostly plains, they may not be in use. Or they actually still could be because it's still a fast way to get around.

As long as we have a justification that makes sense, we can do what we want here. Sometimes it's a good idea to have variety for not only different kinds of terrain, but different kinds of skillsets and peoples found there.

OUR POWER'S REPUTATION

The last subject I want to cover before we close out and talk about where to start is the reputation of our sovereign power. All countries have a reputation for one thing or another. A single dictatorship might have the same reputation among two different democracies, or it might have different ones. More importantly, a dictatorship will view a dictatorship differently than a democracy will view that dictatorship. Now, if that's starting to seem like a lot of work to make up all those viewpoints and reputations among different ones, we don't really need to do that. We just need to do the one that we're going to actually use.

Granted, if we have a character from a democracy and a character from a dictatorship who have become friends, and they're approaching another dictatorship, each one of them might have a different attitude about what's going on there and what the reputation of that place is. But this is not a scenario that we usually use. That's the scenario where you are going to have to worry about this. So, I'm going to read off a quick list here of things that a country might have a reputation for.

One of them could be a mad king. It could be slavery, whether they have slaves or whether they are the source of exported slaves. It could have a reputation for space-craft design or a type of man-o-war ship. Maybe it's a repu-tation for raiders, like the Vikings, or conquerors, individuals like Genghis Khan. Maybe there are unique plants and animals or products, or a war that seems to nev-er end. It could be known for superior weapons, armor, technology or other devices. And they could have really powerful wizards, or maybe wizards are banned altogether in that sovereign power. So, you can make up your own list of things that we can give a reputation for, and these are things that we might want to choose based on the story that we are going to tell.

WHERE TO START

So, let's conclude by talking about where to start. Creating a sovereign power is a really big subject. So much so that it has taken three different podcast episodes to cover much of what is included in the *Creating Life* book about this. And there are some things that I did not cover. When get-ting started, we can often do things in different orders, but, I think, with a sovereign power, we should first decide on a very big picture item, which is, this supposed to be a force for good or for evil? Because that's probably one of the two ways we're going to use it.

Once we decide this, we can then choose the form of government because a force for evil is going to have a more restrictive, authoritarian government, and a force for good is most likely going to have a more democratic one. Next, we should really think about where on the continent it lies because that's going to determine any other sovereign powers that we've already invented and the kinds of conflicts that are going on between them. It's also going to determine what land features are included or near that sovereign power. And that, in turn, will also impact what kind of resources that are there, and potentially some of the conflicts and the population makeup in different parts of our sovereign power and overall.

And, lastly, we can start worrying about some of the simpler items like the identifiers, the customs and the languages that are found there. Creating a sovereign power is actually one of the more fun things if you have a pretty good idea on how to go about it. And I would recommend signing up for *The Art of World Building* newsletter, if you haven't already, and getting the free template that walks you through filling out all of this.

HOW TO CREATE
A SETTLEMENT

H ello and welcome to *The Art of World Building Pod-cast*, episode number fifteen, part 1. Today's topic is how to create a settlement. This includes the impact of location, population, zoning, its history, and any secrets it holds. This material and more is discussed in chapter 6 of *Creating Places*, volume 2 in *The Art of World Building* book series.

LOCATION

One of the most important aspects of any settlement is its location because that determines so many things about what happens there. This includes the reason it exists on that spot, to what it has to defend itself against, the climate, species, culture and a lot more. So, we're going to start with this. First, we'll talk about climate, and we'll only touch on this briefly because we already did a whole episode about this earlier. Today, we just want to talk about how this affects our settlement.

Climate is a consistent weather pattern over a long period of time, and it affects the amount of rainfall, the temperature and the air quality. Since the climate generally stays the same in a place for thousands of years, any city built there is going to experience that climate for a long time and adjust to that climate. This not only affects the people there and the culture that develops, but it also affects the plants and the animals who live there, or nearby, and that, in turn, affects the livestock and anything else that's available for the people who live there.

A simple example of this is that some climates cause a desert to form and other climates cause a rainforest, and these are basically the opposite of each other when it comes to rain and how much livestock and plant life is found there. That's an especially dramatic example, but less dramatic versions of this happen, such as one area of the United States is known for being really humid and hot, but another area of it is known for being really hot, but dry. And the result is that people think of these places different ways, even if they don't live there, just because they've heard of what life is like there. They hear about it because it's important to the people who live there and it has affected the way they live their lives. For example, in the hot and humid area, people probably don't spend quite as much time outdoors during the summer. We could think of many examples of this, but you can really just base things on analogues. Something from Earth.

One of the great things about deciding our climate is that if we have a map, for example, and we've already decided where our city is located, our map may have already basically told us what the climate there is. In that sense, the work is done for us. Now, if we don't have a map, we may want to choose a city that we are familiar with, or at least one that we've heard about, and choose to use that as the basis as far as the climate goes, and then research that city on the internet and see what life is like there as far as how that climate affects people.

When we first go to create a settlement, all we really need is a high-level idea of what it is like, such as humid or dry, rainy or arid, hot or cold. More details than that are something that we can add later. Also bear in mind that the terrain can affect the climate because if we have a city that is very high in the mountains, for example, the climate is going to be different there than we might expect, given the latitude where it is found. This is also something that we discussed in a previous episode.

TERRAIN

This is a good segue into talking about terrain, so let's focus on that. If our settlement is located in the mountains, those mountains are going to inhibit travel to and from that settlement over land. If we have a science fiction setting, or even a fantasy one where there are a lot of giant birds of prey or dragons or something similar that flies, some of this could be mitigated. Keep this level of technology in mind when you are laying out a mountainous settlement because, depending on how much ability there is to go over walls and over the terrain, this will impact the kind of fortifications that they have, and that's something that we'll talk a little more about in the next episode.

What you want to do in the beginning is get a feel for how well-visited is this place? Do they seldom see travelers, or are travelers coming there all the time anyway? Decide how easy it is for people to get there. Also consider how technology has changed. It might be that in the past there wasn't technology that allowed people to easily get there, and, as a result, there weren't too much in the way of walls, but now it is easy for people to get there via the air and there still aren't too many reasons for walls. But maybe they have other fortifications instead.

Part of what we're getting at here is that there might be fortifications that are old and in disrepair because they no longer apply, such as a wall that used to keep people out, but now technology has rendered that well meaningless, but no one took the time to knock it down, so it's still standing. Maybe sections of it have fallen down and no one has done anything about it. This is the kind of thing that we can use to characterize the age of a place as people are arriving, or if we're just setting our entire story there.

Another thing to keep in mind with mountains is that this will really limit where any farmland is, and might inhibit it altogether, depending on how rugged that terrain is. Keep in mind that mountain ranges typically have valleys and those may be wide enough and fertile enough for farmland. However, this does restrict them to that particular valley and, as a result, there is some vulnerability to someone burning down the crops or just predators knowing that our species are there and they can be attacked because they're working the land at times.

A mountainous settlement is also a likely one to have a certain amount of involvement in mining. This is going to help us think of some potential products that they might have in the form of gemstones or other materials that they've pulled out of the earth. The settlement might even be rich because of this. Maybe they have big walls after all.

Bear in mind that any settlement might be adjacent to more than one terrain. So, for example, with a desert city, we don't have to decide that it's entirely in the desert. We could just have the desert be off to one side. Now, there's not going to be a lush forest right next to a desert because, if you've been paying attention to these episodes, that's not typically the way climate works unless something like magic is at play.

We could also use technology because, certainly in our modern times, we have turned entire deserts into something that's got enough vegetation for people to live. In a futuristic society, we could certainly do the same. The real point I'm getting at here is that by having more than one terrain type near our settlement, we can make use of more than one. This gives us the best of both worlds, and potentially the worst of both worlds. You may recall from a previous episode that not all deserts are actually sandy. Many of them are hard. But let's say, for the sake of argument, that we have a sandy desert to one side. It's unlikely that an army is going to choose to approach from that direction. On the other hand, if there are grasslands in the other direction, that's probably the way they're going to come. This may have an impact on the internal layout of our city, not to mention the fortifications.

Another terrain type that might be near, but not surrounding, our settlement is a forest. Fortifications is one of the basic reasons for this because a forest can hide an approaching army. It's fairly standard for the inhabitants of that settlement to cut down the trees within a certain distance around the settlement, such as a mile or two. So, even if our settlement is inside the forest completely, there's still going to be that cleared area around it. But we may want to just decide to put our settlement adjacent to that forest.

One great thing about a forest is that the trees and the other plants there provide a great number of products that our people are going to use for one thing or another, such as building ships. There's more mundane stuff that they can do with it, but I think the presence of wooden ships in a fantasy setting is something that's pretty important. This can greatly expand how far people can go, but the absence of those will also restrict them from going anywhere. This is something to keep in mind. Just as with mountains, we need to figure out how often is this place visited, or how often do people travel away from here to other places? We need to do this with other settlements, whether or not they have a forest and access to water, whether that's the ocean, a lake or even a river.

A water source is another thing that's really important, not only for the ability to drink it, but because of these travel opportunities. Anywhere that's located on a coastline, such as the ocean or a large lake, is going to be visited and also have the ability to travel, assuming that there is a forest nearby for them to create ships from.

Some of these settlements near the water might also have other dangers that they face, just like in the mountains we might have something that's living underground and that comes out from time to time. Near a large water source, we could, of course, have sea monsters. We may have also chosen to invent species that are water-dwelling and which are sentient, and therefore can interact with our species. So, by knowing that these exist and deciding where our settlement is, we can decide whether that species is well-known there or not.

Bear in mind that there are underground rivers, and these could allow a species that is water-dwelling to get much further inland than we might expect them to. There are a lot of products that come from the sea, and I'm not just talking about food. This could be anything like candle wax from whales, to any product that we invent.

Another subject we should think about is whether the terrain is impacting the layout of our city. This is something that's certainly going to happen in the mountains because if there's a giant area of hard ground, we just aren't going to be building anything on that. We may want to decide that there's a large outcropping of rock that's in the middle of a settlement, and that it acts as some sort of gathering place for people. It could also be a convenient lookout point when people climb it, or it could also be used for games such as those by adolescents.

Higher areas are typically used for defense, such as a castle being built there. Sometimes this is also where wealthier people will live. Water is generally considered to be more advantageous than not having the water. And I don't mean on the grand scale, but just that the wealthy people will be those more likely to live near a river, for example. This isn't always true because it will depend on the river and other factors, but it's something to keep in mind as an option. On the other hand, the port area of a town is going to be a little more rundown in many cases, but it will depend on the settlement and what you want to do. In a fantasy world, it is often shown that a port is somewhere where nefarious people are more likely to gather, such as pickpockets and those without a job. On the other hand, in certain modern ports here on Earth, we have very nice ports where that have been turned into a tourist destination.

Bear in mind that something like a river can act like a natural mote, preventing or inhibiting an army from attacking from that side. And, obviously, a big body of water is going to have the same affect, unless, of course, they are attacking from wooden ships. Well, in a fantasy setting, they will be wooden. But, of course, they don't have to be. Generally, you want to figure out how the terrain has impacted the layout of your city. Where's the river or lake? Where are the higher areas? Is there something that must be built around, and what is it? Is it a swampy area or is it a giant boulder? Variation is good.

WATER SUPPLY AND OLD TOWN

We should also consider where the water supply is and remember that seawater cannot be consumed by humans, at least, because the salt will make us sick. Our basic options are a river, lake, spring or well. In a more modern or futuristic society, we could have giant stations that are basically turning seawater into something that is drinkable, because that is possible, even today. That process is called desalinization. When laying out our settlement, it helps to know where that water supply is. If we have a settlement that is a large town, or even bigger, such as a city, then there's probably going to be an area that's called "Old Town," or something similar. Old Town is definitely going to have its own water source. After all, that's where people started building this place.

Just like we were talking about with ports, Old Town can sometimes be a rundown area that is not much traveled, or it can be a tourist destination that is well kept. As you build many settlements across one world or multiple worlds, try to vary this. Regardless, Old Town tends to be a place with narrower streets and where the buildings are kind of crowded in close upon each other. So, decide if there is an Old Town, where it's located, and what it's like.

THE NEIGHBORS

We should also think about who the neighbors are. This can include sovereign powers. After all, our settlement is either deep within a sovereign power, near the edge of its power, or in a land without a power ruling it. If it's deep within a territory, it's not going to be reached quickly by an invading army. This means it might enjoy more peace of mind, and therefore have less expectations of war. In fact, the population there could be rather skeptical of ever being attacked. They might be complacent. This does depend on the strength of the sovereign power to whom it belongs, because if it's a new power or one that is actually failing in some way due to something like famine, or just poor government, then that kind of weakness can invite another sovereign power to attack. It's also possible that the settlement is now deep within a territory, but that sometime in its past it was closer towards the border. This is another scenario where it might have walls for fortifications, but those are not necessarily being kept that well anymore. Maybe the guards who are on those walls are just doing a kind of duty where they don't expect any actual fighting.

If the settlement has been near the border of a sovereign power, that means it might have been attacked repeatedly over the coarse of it's history by another sovereign power's cities. If it's currently near a border, then that means it's probably built up a little bit more when it comes to military and fortifications. And it might even have people who specialize in certain kinds of fighting, such as if we have a kind of species that is known to live in that neighboring sovereign power, we might have people who are good at fighting that.

During either times of peace or war, it's possible that people could come to this settlement for training, and that could be something that we make our settlement known for. This is one way in which the neighbors can help build up our city. So, one of the things we need to decide is where inside our sovereign power is this settlement, and how long has it been there? If it was part of another sovereign power, and that has a very different culture, we can also then figure out what cultural elements from that other sovereign power have impacted this one.

Another option we have is a city or city state that is not part of a sovereign power. Some such places might be very strong, but others could be very vulnerable. Decide if this place needs allies and whether or not it has them, and from where. That will determine how quickly someone can come to their aid. It's also possible that one of its allied cities is the one that has been captured recently by another sovereign power, and now cannot come to its aid. Many places will have been conquered at some time in their past, so it helps to figure out how long ago this last happened, how often it happens, and how did it end? Is this settlement recently captured or was that a long time ago and it's at peace with being part of whatever sovereign power it now is part of? Or is this settlement a little bit restless as far as the population, and they would like to have their freedom back but they don't think there is anything they can do? Maybe everyone is just biding their time.

For any settlement that's within a sovereign power, we can generally assume that other settlements within that sovereign power are basically friendly toward it. However, this may not be true if they were once adversaries or at least recently so, especially if there's another nearby settlement that has only been recently conquered by the sovereign power to which our current settlement belongs. One thing I'm getting at here is trying to create a little bit of history for our settlement. We don't have to explain history, but we can show it in various ways, such as architecture that came from another sovereign power that is no longer ruling this place.

Our characters may be aware of such a thing, and we could have them walking down the street and see a building that they despise because of that association. Maybe they think about this as they're going. We'll only want to do this if it impacts the scene that we're telling, but there are ways to do that. For example, maybe he's about to meet another character who is from that sovereign power.

I've already mentioned that there could be skilled warriors here due to threats that this settlement faces, but we're also going to have skilled laborers who have one talent or another based on the kind of terrain that is nearby. For example, if the right kinds of trees are nearby, we're going to have people who are good at building ships. If there are mountains here, we might have a mining colony and we could have people who are good at carving those stones.

Think about who is here, and why. And one of the reasons we can do this is that our characters are going to have some sort of history or a family business that they have originated from. Even if our character is now an adventurer, for example, and he's going to go out and do whatever adventurers do, his family probably has a business that they run, or that they're at least part of. What is this guy trying to get away from? What talents does he have that he almost wishes he didn't have, but he was forced to acquire those by his parents? You can see there are ways to tie all of this together.

We should also decide on a very important set of skills, and that is who are the warriors, healers, wizards and something like fighter pilots, and do they come from the settlement or not?

POPULATION

We've already begun to discuss population, but I think there's more that we can dive into here. One of the subjects is which species are here. In fantasy, in particular, there's a tendency to present one city as being all human, another as all dwarven, another as elven, but there isn't too much of a mix being shown. This seems like an oversight, and it is usually justified by saying that each one of these species has some sort of attitude about the others. While that is true, it's a bit of a cliche, and it might be more interesting to have more of a melting pot going on. Now, some people might automatically assume that if there is a melting pot, that people are getting along so much better and that we have eliminated some source of conflict. But if you put people together, there could actually be more conflict. And if we look at a country like the United States, we are one of the biggest melting pots in the world and we certainly have all sorts of racial conflict here.

In SF, it seems to be more common that we have a mix, and this might be because we are typically showing places where so many different planets and cultures within those planets have the ability to travel through space and they end up mingling much more. Regardless of how big a melting pot concept we decide to do, one of the species is still going to be a majority. We should decide who that is, and when we're trying to figure out which other species live here and in what percentages, we should consider those land features we already talked about.

I'm going to use fantasy as an example because it's a little more consistent with the races that are there, but if you have mountains nearby, then you're going to have dwarves as part of this settlement. The same is true with forests and elves. Some of these land features might be close enough that we see these species all the time. Maybe not that many of them live here, but quite a few of them would and they would certainly be frequent visitors. And if they're all part of the same sovereign power, then, in theory, they get along. By "get along," I mean that they are not starting wars with each other. They might still have bar fights, but that's not the same thing.

Now, whether we use the standard fantasy races or make up our own, we might want to decide that they are not so stuck on this idea that the dwarves only live under mountains and they don't venture out except for adventures or short periods, and the same with elves. Why not have them be people who are willing to form a joint settlement with other species? This gives us another variety, and variety is good. We can have different things going on in different parts of the world. Maybe there's a forest with elves who are very opposed to outsiders, and they keep to themselves like the stereotype. But then maybe we have another forest full of a different elven population that is much more gregarious and outgoing.

There's also work that people can have. So, for example, dwarves are supposed to be really good at cutting through stone, so wouldn't they be in high demand in a city that is somewhere else and that skill is needed? Maybe by dwarven standards, this character is not considered really good, and therefore he's been denied the right to do this for a living. So, he leaves and he goes to a mostly human settlement, and there he's considered some sort of amazing expert, even though back home he's not.

We can find ways like this to make our species more intermingled. If we have something like a monarchy, a kingdom, we could have this situation where only the humans are allowed to be part of the royal family, and therefore in the ruling class. But what about a democracy? That form of government is supposed to be by the people and for the people, and if we have a significant population of our different species living here, then shouldn't they be represented in that government? In that case, you would have a situation where someone like an elf could be elected in a human settlement. Now, maybe it won't happen due to politics and all of that, but it should be possible.

Another thing to keep in mind is that forms of government change. So, we could've had a form of government at one point, and as, let's say, 100 years passed, more and more elves are becoming part of the population. Then that government type falls and is replaced by, let's say, a democracy. And now the elves are a significant percentage, and they manage to acquire more power than they once had. This is a believable scenario because populations of any city or a sovereign power slowly change over time. I can tell that I have sovereign powers on my mind because some of what I was saying kind of applies a little bit more to that than to settlements. But, of course, I just did three episodes on sovereign powers.

Regardless, the idea still holds true. We should have a population that is a little bit more mixed in at least some of the settlements that we create. We can certainly have restaurants that cater to certain populations. Here in the United States, we have Japanese restaurants, Chinese and all this other stuff. Why not have the same thing where you have elven restaurants and dwarven restaurants? Why can't we have a situation where a human character really likes elven food and goes to eat at the elven restaurant all the time? Maybe he's on friendly terms with the elves, and that this was how that got started. Maybe another character hates elves and refuses to eat such food.

Something I'm not going to cover here too much are who the leaders of this settlement really are. This detail, and a bunch of other stuff, is covered a lot more in *Creating Places*, but one of the things that is discussed there is who the leader is and what the power structure is among that leader and the other people who are responsible for running the town. This is something that our characters need to know because if they are traveling and they arrive in this settlement, they need to know who they're dealing with and how much power that person really has.

In our modern world, we tend to ignore that sort of thing, but there are certainly people who pay more attention to it. And I think in a more fantasy-like setting where people are traveling and there is not so much of a homogenous country where so many things are the same and these basics are taken for granted, people tend to pay more attention to what kind of power the mayor has, for example. By contrast, I don't even know who the mayor of my city is. I certainly don't know what kind of power he has because it doesn't really seem to come up or affect me in any way. I suspect that for many of you this is the same.

We should also think about who has influence, because there may be someone who is basically corrupting an official in some way, such as either bribery or having compromising information on that person. Our characters may arrive in this settlement and learn that certain person has power and that they should be able to do something, but they actually can't and they're not going to admit it because they don't want to talk about the compromise that someone has placed on them.

There might also be other important people here, such as a hero or a wizard, or someone from the past who has done something and acquired a reputation. There could be monuments to such a person around town. If our characters are from the settlement that we're creating, then this is something that they would be aware of. Maybe this settlement is a small village or small town and people are well aware of that's where a certain hero came from, and therefore they're curious and then maybe they're disappointed when they arrive there. It's also possible for villains to be calling this their home, and that might be openly or it might not be openly. Perhaps this is the person who has compromising information on the mayor.

We should think about the overall disposition of our population. Small towns can sometimes be romanticized as being a wonderful place that has no evil, but, on the other hand, everyone knows everyone else's business. A large city is a little different in that you might never even meet someone who lives there, despite living there your entire life. But there are also good things and bad things about this, such as the higher quality of goods and other merchandise just because there is so much competition.

When we are creating multiple settlements, we might want to decide on a different disposition to the population for each one. We should decide on the general feel, such as whether it's dangerous of safe, whether it's kind of boring, or if it's maybe a sleepy or bustling town, or is it transient in that people are coming through there all the time, or is the population very stable? Is it easy or hard to reach? Is it welcoming to people or not? It could be a rich settlement or a poor one. Is it artful? Is it high-minded or is it down to earth? When we're making up our mind here, we don't really need a reason to decide that it is one way versus another, but if we do want to reason, we should consider what surrounds that settlement.

For example, a remote town might feel safe, stable, poor, sleepy and down to earth, and maybe even religious with less technology. A built-up city is more likely to be a little bit dangerous, it's going to be bustling, there's going to be more transients of people coming and going, it might be welcoming or indifferent to visitors and travelers, and it will be richer in some areas and poorer in others. It's also probably going to have more technology.

There's another idea that I like, and that is a quarter. You have probably heard of the French Quarter in New Orleans. This does not mean that French people live there, but I'm going to use that basic idea. We could have a mostly human city that has an elven quarter or a dwarven quarter, and where those populations are typically found in that quarter because buildings and other things there, like the architecture and just the way things look and feel and the size, is all based on that species and caters to them. If you like this idea, decide if your settlement has such an area.

ZONING

Another concept to be aware of is that of zoning. What this means is that residential, commercial, industrial and agricultural zones are often created in settlements to separate things. If you've ever played a game like Sim City, you have some familiarity with this because if you create something like the garbage dump that's needed to take care of the city's waste and you put it too close to the residential areas, the game will start telling you your characters are unhappy in that residential area because they just smell the garbage all the time. So, you're supposed to try to layout your city so that there's not an overlap of certain things. This is a simple subject, but it's something that's sort of advanced in the sense that you don't really need to worry about this too much unless you are taking the time to draw a map of your settlement.

Now, if you would like to sketch something that no one sees just so you can get a better sense of how things are laid out, this is a good idea. We've already talked about several areas to be aware of, such as where Old Town is, where the source of water is, if there's a river or something, if there is an area that has high ground, or if there's some sort of obstacle like a giant outcropping of rock.

Another area to consider is where are these different zones? When I do this, I first think about where I would like people to live, and then I put the commercial stuff nearby and I put the industrial stuff just a little bit further away. It's tempting to say that the wealthy people are in one area and the poorer people are in another, and that does happen, but sometimes they are mixed together. This is arguably better for conflict. The upper class might also be farther upstream because all the refuse will flow downstream towards the poorer people. This is one of the things that wealth gets you.

SECRETS

We should also consider what secrets there might be in this town and if those have anything to do with this physical location. We can also decide what sort of secrets our settlement has. Some of these might be based on its location. Secrets could be incorporated into this city layout that we've been talking about. For example, maybe there are catacombs or some other supernatural phenomenon that's underground and a building has built over that location. And over the centuries, most people have forgotten that this is there, or maybe they never knew at all. If we have gods or world figures or even the undead, we can create these places that have some sort of significance.

Secrets can be a little bit more mundane, such as some sort of nasty group that is operating out of this settlement. What comes to mind on Earth is terrorist groups. Naturally, these groups don't invent a settlement. They find one that is welcoming in some way, or at least allows them to operate. Consider what sort of secrets there might be here, and if you were to read *Creating Places*, Chapter 11 is called "Creating Places of Interest," and it has more ideas.

In Closing

That's going to be all for today's episode. In our next one, we will continue our discussion on how to create a settlement and we're going to tackle a really big subject. That's going to be the differences between a village, town, city and megalopolis. Each of these has their own consideration and things that are possible there and things which are not. We'll also talk a little more in detail about the defense of these places, how a settlement is known, and how many places you should create.

HOW TO CREATE
A SETTLEMENT

Hello and welcome to *The Art of World Building Podcast*, episode number fifteen, part two. Today's topic concludes our discussion about how to create a settlement. This includes the differences between an outpost, village, town, city, and even settlements in space. This material and more is discussed in chapter 6 of *Creating Places*, volume 2 in *The Art of World Building* book series.

THE OUTPOST

When we're populating our continent with settlement types, we have a variety of these to choose from, and we're going to start this podcast by starting with the smallest ones, like an outpost, and work our way up to the megalopolis. The difference between all of them is, of course, physical, and this is determined, partly, by population size, their defenses and the availability of resources. But size, in turn, affects what is available there.

We can call something an outpost, a castle, a tower or something else, but we're talking about a single building or a small group of them that are not big enough to qualify as a village. I'm generalizing throughout this episode, but these outposts may not be permanently staffed. This may have consequences, such as the inability to do farm work, depending on how often this place is inhabited.

Naturally, once plants are planted, they need time to grow and, arguably, there's only so much that needs to happen in the meantime. Now, someone who is a farmer listening to this might think that there's all sorts of things that need to happen, so pardon my ignorance, but if there are people there every season and they can do something with the plants that have been planted, such as harvesting them or planting them at a different time, then it may be possible for farming to happen. But my point is that if no one is there except for occasionally, such as once a year, then farming is not going to happen.

Farming is not the most exciting topic to most of us, but the point here is that if people cannot grow their food there, they're going to have to bring it in from somewhere else. In science fiction, with something like a food replicator, this is less of an issue. In a fantasy setting with magic, it might be possible to open a portal somewhere and, therefore, supplies can come in that way. Without these options, people are going to have to bring their food with them. The exception is, of course, anything that they can catch or hunt.

Now, to over simply things, if the inhabitants are basically evil and they do obnoxious things, then they're not going to have any problem raiding a local village or town for their food supplies. On the other hand, if they're more benevolent and get along with people, and this is part of a sovereign power and there is a nearby village, town or whatever, then that other settlement might be tasked with providing food as necessary to anyone who is in this outpost. Another option here is that this outpost could be so far away from every other settlement, and it might even be forgotten, that there is no one who is responsible for this place. And that's true whether we're talking about supplies or even maintaining this place when no one is occupying it.

If no one is responsible for this place, then it has probably fallen into a certain amount of disrepair. Another option we have is that there might be other things inhabiting it. For example, we could have a monster living there. We could have orcs, goblins or something else in a typical fantasy setting that are making use of this settlement. This might be a known problem so that anyone who is intending to come there and make use of this for more peaceful purposes, for example, they might know that when they arrive they're going to have to fight and drive out anything that is occupying it.

Some of these considerations are things that we can do to make it seem like this is not just a standing building that's out there and no one has anything to do with it and it's not connected to the real world. There are people and things that are going to be using this even if no one is consistently using it. Some of these might have been truly abandoned so that they are a ruin, but other ones might be only temporarily used or maybe only used seasonally. If that's the case, you're probably going to need a reason for that. For example, using weather, let's say that there's a monsoon season that only takes place for about two months in every year and, during that time, the monsoon causes certain things to happen to the land. As a result, this place should be occupied. In preparation for the upcoming monsoon season, people will probably come here and clear out anything living there and spruce it up a little bit.

Another issue is that the population is smaller and, therefore, there are a lot of professions who are not actually present. In fantasy, they might realize they need a carpenter or a blacksmith, but one is not present. In science fiction, they may realize they need someone with technical skills, like an engineer, and this person simply isn't present, or the one they have is not advanced enough to do what is needed. This is one reason such an outpost could have an alliance with a larger settlement. There's also likely to be no police force here so that someone is taking it upon themselves to deal with such matters if it comes up.

When creating an outpost and deciding which professions are not here, try to think of something where the absence of that person is going to cause a problem for your story. An obvious example would be medical personnel. If someone gets hurt, it's a little too easy for us to think of the perfect healing ability or technology to fully recover that person. It might be better to have them still impaired in some way, but not as bad as when they were first wounded. Try not to make everything too easy for them.

CASTLES

Arguably, the largest outpost is going to be something like a castle that has no village surrounding it. Castles are defensive in nature and, therefore, they are largely self-sufficient. They will need the farmland nearby, but of course, a certain amount of those supplies are stored within the castle so that they can withstand a siege of a certain duration, such as a month. However, until recently, the ability to preserve food is pretty limited. So, don't think that you're going to have a castle where they have like a year's worth of food and it's not going to just rot within a month. That's only likely to happen if magic is involved.

Now, there may be buildings adjacent to this castle that are not big enough to be considered a village, but basically, these are temporary buildings in the sense that they could be destroyed during a siege, and it's not a huge loss to the people in the castle. They can always rebuild those. So, there's only going to be so many of them in this scenario we're talking about where there's a castle with no real village. There may still be these other buildings around.

One big question for world builders is where do we place a castle? These are typically placed along an important trade route. They may be near a dangerous territory, such as a mountain pass. If there are nasty things like ogres in that mountain range and they are likely to emerge from those mountains in that mountain pass, then somewhere within a mile or two of that pass there's probably going to be a castle. The idea would be to stop these ogres before they get further into a sovereign power.

This has another advantage to us in that we can decide that we have a character who is something like a knight who has special training in fighting ogres. And how did he acquire that training? Well, he went to live in that castle for a couple years and he specialized in doing this because that's what goes on there. This castle could be famous for that and any knight who lives there should be required to go there. And this is one way we can fill out the backstory for such a character.

Another thing to consider about castle placement is that, yes, we may have decided that we want one within, say, two miles of this mountain pass, or whatever the danger is, but then the question is, well, where within those two miles do they actually build the castle? Since it is defensive in nature, castles are often built on existing areas of land that have some sort of natural fortification. The easiest of those is land that is simply higher than the surrounding terrain. There might be something like a cliff face that is standing behind this castle so that no one can attack from behind. There could be a body of water there that is large enough to inhibit anyone from attacking the castle from that direction. If there's a cliff face on one side and a body of water on another, then this place can only be attacked from two different directions.

A final word on castles is that there seems to be an oversight in a lot of fiction where if a castle is located within a sovereign power, but near the border – and we're talking like 50 miles – then there is this impression that whoever owns that castle now has always owned it and, therefore, they are the only ones who know the secrets of this castle. Well, the reality is that if this castle has stood for, say, 1,000 years, it has probably changed hands several times, especially if it is near a border like that.

I can tell you this: If I captured your castle, I would do everything I could to learn its secrets. And then if, let's say 50 years later, my country lost that castle to yours again, well, I would still know those secrets. I mean, I might be dead. But the point is my sovereign power, we would still understand the secrets of your castle. So, we might know how to break into it in some sort of secret avenue that you've created, such as hidden tunnels or whatever. So, it's not going to be the situation where I don't have any tactical knowledge of your castle. I'm probably going to know a lot about it. So, try not to fall into this trap of portraying your characters in a story as being the only ones who understand the secrets of this castle. That's probably not true.

VILLAGES

Let's talk villages. When we are going to create a settlement type, we often are trying to figure out, "Should it be a village, a city, a town or what?" If we have a map and there's an area that we consider to be somewhat out of the way, but potentially useful, this is where we might choose to place a village. Why a village? Well, because we might reason that this place has some things to offer, but not so many that it's going to attract a lot of people. Generally, you probably want to place your villages on a map after you have already decided where the major cities are. Actually, to be honest, I don't even place villages on my maps unless I'm doing something really regional. The reason is that there would be so many villages that it would completely consume my map. That's all you would see.

Even so, this basic idea of an out-of-the-way village is one to keep in mind. Such a place is probably less visited and, therefore, they might be less likely to be welcoming of strangers or travelers, and this is something to keep in mind if your characters are going to arrive there. They are more likely to be viewed with suspicion.

Another location for a village is along an important trade route, but not at a critical part of that trade route. At a more critical location, such as a place where multiple roads are coming together from different directions, that might be a major trading point that increasingly builds up to a town and then, later, a city.

So, if we have something like a city at a major crossroads, then where would the villages be? Well, they're going to be along those trade routes, but at not such a critical place. By along the trade route, I don't mean that they're necessarily right on the road. They could be several miles off to one side. They are, once again, going to be somewhat remote, but not as remote as one that is off in the middle of nowhere. They, therefore, might be used to travelers, especially if it actually is built along the road and it can be seen from there. Such a place is more likely welcoming of strangers.

In the *Creating Places* book, I have an entire chapter about travel on land, and one of the things you learn in that chapter is how long it takes to get from one place to another by various means of locomotion. The reason I mention this is that if two locations are within a day's travel, there's probably not going to be a village along the way. On the other hand, if it would take a week to go from one major location to another, then there's probably going to be something like a village or a town in between. The reason for this is not only the distance that needs to be traveled, and the fact that a certain number of people are going to be living there, but the reality is that people need somewhere to stay overnight when they are traveling by land. A village may spring up for exactly that purpose. Now, originally, it's probably just something like a campsite that has a convenient water access. In time, maybe someone built an inn or a tavern there and this becomes the focal point of a village that slowly grows out from around it.

For example, if wagons are routinely going through there, well, wagons breakdown. We might need a carpenter and a blacksmith. So, these might be two people who live in that town. Well, we're talking villages, but you know what I mean. This sort of point of origin is a good idea to keep in mind because it can affect the attitude of our settlement, such as whether they are welcoming of strangers or they don't want them to come there. There are other ways that the attitude of such a place can be affected by this. An out-of-the-way village might be one where everyone shares a similar religious belief, for example. Differences might be less tolerated.

By contrast, a village with a more transient population of people coming and going through there is going to be more tolerant of differences. If I'm a traveler and I'm about to approach a village that's in an out-of-the-way location, maybe I'm smart enough to hide something like a talisman of the god that I worship because I don't know if that is viewed favorably there. On the other hand, if I'm approaching a village that is right along a major trade route, I might reasonably assume that they are more tolerant and not do such a thing.

Another thing to keep in mind with all villages is that they are less likely to have a dedicated, official protector like a sheriff. The community might be small enough to not need someone who does that on a full-time basis. The reason we might care about this is that there's probably someone in that settlement who is a better fighter than everyone else, such as an expert swordsman, for example, and that person is the one who is looked to by the rest of the villagers for guidance or, at least, interference when there's some sort of fight that breaks out. Or if villagers are being approached by travelers who are coming there, this might be the person who someone goes running to get and says, "Hey, there are some people coming up on horses," for example. "Why don't you come up in a show of strength and make it clear, 'Hey, we're not just defenseless villagers. We've got a guy here with a sword and he looks like he knows what he's doing.'"

So, this person might be seen as an unofficial protector of the town. The same can be done in science fiction where a character can just appear to have a lot of confidence with the way they wear their guns or they've got some sort of rifle slung over their back. A village is also unlikely to have something like a wall surrounding it. Or, if they do, it's probably going to be made of something like wood. That may be less true in science fiction because they are more likely to have technology in general, and it's relatively easy to have something like a wall built if you have things like spaceships. And, of course, that wall is not going to be made of wood.

While a village may have characters like a carpenter or a blacksmith or an engineer in science fiction, they may not have these individuals. So, once again, we might decide who is here and who is not. The big reason I mention this is that, let's say it's fantasy and there used to be a blacksmith who lived here, but he recently died six months ago. Well, now things might be falling into disrepair a little bit and one of our visiting characters might have that skill and be able to barter that. In other words, maybe this character doesn't have money to pay for food and lodging, but they have the skill and they might have to stay for a week doing a bunch of repairs. And the same thing can be done in science fiction with an engineer.

TOWNS

Let's talk about towns. Unlike with the villages, a town is likely to have more than one of something, such as a blacksmith, a carpenter or an engineer. This means that not only is the population not going to be deprived of such expertise, but there is competition for these people's skills and the business. A side effect of competition is that everyone raises their game. The result is that everyone here is likely to have a superior skillset compared to the same people who are from a village. Our traveling characters are also less likely to get away with bartering their services for fare and lodging. In other words, they're going to need money. If they don't have any, this might be one reason why they visit villages instead of towns.

Another issue with a town is that there tends to be more diversity of the population, and this includes races and species. Depending on which ones you have invented or included in your settlement, this might also affect the amount of crime that takes place here. For that reason, some species might not be welcome here. Or, if they are, they are watched very carefully, or there might be special rules just for them. These rules can include a curfew or not being allowed to carry weapons. There is also almost certainly a dedicated police force. Both promote more rules and laws. That, in turn, means there's probably a jail.

Now, there are likely to be fewer laws here than a city, which means that there could be more corruption. We could have businesses more likely to cheat customers, for example. Sometimes corrupt officials hold considerable power, and this kind of reminds me a lot of the Hollywood westerns that we've seen. A stereotype of those is a traveling character who arrives somewhere and runs afoul of the corrupt sheriff who is intimidating the town.

Taxes are almost a certainty in a town. While that's not a glamorous subject, one of the things that comes with taxes is the ability for the town itself to improve the town. This could mean better roads and better fortifications. Those police we were just talking about need to be paid. We don't really need to worry about what taxes are used for, but the basic idea is that the town tends to be better quality precisely because of the taxes. There's also a kind of infrastructure there in the sense that there might be a mayor and he needs to make a living. Although, in some places, he may not be officially paid.

Generally, things are more official and formal here. Naturally, due to the population size, there's going to be a lot more farming going on nearby. In a less civilized world, like in a fantasy, the farmers may have a lot of prominence. Whereas, in our modern world, we tend to take that for granted because we have such an abundance of food. Try to keep this in mind if you're writing such a scenario because the farmers have a lot of power.

In addition to the mayor, there might also be a formal town counsel. These people might be appointed, but they might also just be people who have influence in some way, such as those farmers we were just talking about. We could have a wizard, a blacksmith, an engineer or whoever we think is important to this town's functioning.

A town often has one or more families that have been there a really long time, and they are considered to be very influential and, in fact, the town might actually bear one of their names. In order to ease the management of a town, it is sometimes divided up into wards, with each one of those neighborhoods having someone who is ostensibly in charge of that ward. Those individuals are the ones who can be voted on and voted into the town counsel to represent the interests of that ward.

Another issue with a town is that there may be zoning. What I mean is residential, commercial and industrial areas. If you've ever played a game like Sim City, you know that it's not a good idea to have your industry right next to your homes because the residents start complaining about the smell, for example. When thinking about laying out the interior of a town, you may want to decide where everything is located.

CITIES

Let's talk about cities. In a place with this many people, there tends to be a lot of formalities such as laws, regulations, police, a legal system, mayors, a voting system in a free society, zoning and even procedures like how to evacuate or handle certain kinds of emergencies. As world builders, we don't typically have to worry about a lot of this and we can simply assume it's there.

However, one area this comes up for is when these laws don't take into account certain minorities who don't have the rights that other people have. This is something we definitely might want to consider because it could impact the lives of our characters whether they live in this city or whether they are just visiting. With visiting characters, some of them may be allowed to carry their weapons while the others have theirs confiscated. Not only can this be based on race or gender, but it can also be based on where this person is from because that other country or city might be a traditional enemy of this one.

Try to think of some restrictions that you can impose on some of your characters, but maybe not all of them. Someone who lives here but is not treated equally might see this as a reason to leave this place for somewhere else. This is one reason why immigrants come to the United States, which is seen as a place where this kind of diversity is more tolerated, even if it is so with limitations. The concept of equality for all is a driving force behind that kind of immigration, even if the reality fails to live up to that.

Cities offer the best and worst of everything because there's a lot of competition here, but there's also a lot of crime. It's going to depend on the settlement, of course, but there's a lot of leeway for people to get away with things. There can be a big difference between how life is for the rich and for the poor.

There's definitely going to be zoning where industrial areas are separated from commercial and residential. It can be tempting to think that the rich people live in one area and that the poor people live in another, but there are certainly places on earth where everyone is mixed up together. So, we have this as an option.

Cities are certainly going to have some of the best fortifications and the military to staff them. It can be assumed that something like a knight from such a place is better trained and has more experience than someone from a town or a village. There is snobbery in all things, so this can also influence the attitude of such a character. Maybe when this guy is traveling and he comes into a village and there's a knight there, he is looking down on that person as being inferior when that person might actually have been from a city or had extensive experience there and is simply living in the village now and is, actually, much more capable than is assumed. This is one of many ways we can add dynamics to our characters.

These military people might have inns, taverns and equipment shops that cater to their needs as well. There may even be a certain amount of culture associated with them because there are so many of them.

There tends to be more anonymity in a city, but that will depend on the technology level. In science fiction, we could easily have people be issued some sort of card that is needed to access every single doorway or something else so that people always know where they are. Without that kind of technology, people are much less likely to know where you are coming and going from because there's simply no way to track you and there are too many people for anyone to be paying too much attention to that.

This is in stark contrast to a village where everyone might know your business, whether you want them to or not. This freedom allows you to do things that might be considered inappropriate. So, let's say that you have a sexual orientation that you don't want anyone to know about. Well, in a village, people are going to figure that out pretty quickly. But in something like a city, it's going to be easier for you to carry on with the kind of relationship that you want, and possibly keep that a secret.

We haven't talked about tolerance since we were talking about villages, but in a city there's likely to be much more tolerance in general of different viewpoints. This does not mean that there's not going to be prejudice. What I mean is that there are going to be individuals who still have a nasty attitude about some other belief system, but all of these belief systems are still there as one giant melting pot where people are mixed together. By contrast, in a village, the people who have some opposing view might actually be shunned out of that village altogether.

In a city, opposing groups with different viewpoints can still be there, but they may not have much interaction with each other. But then, some of them may. So, you'll have a mix of tolerances. Generally, people in a city are exposed to many more ideas that they may not agree with and which may change their opinion about things over time. A generalization we can make about people on earth is that those in cities tend to be exposed to more viewpoints and have more tolerance, while those in more rural areas tend to have a more homogenous viewpoint, and the people who live there are more uniform in the way they think about things. The reasons for that could be complicated, but one of them is just exposure, or lack thereof, to opposing ideas.

The main difference between a city and a megalopolis is simply the size. In our modern world, we have cities that have very large suburbs around them where those suburbs are actually towns. Those towns are often right up against another town that is next to another city so that all of it almost seems like one giant place. Each one of these will still have its own name whether it gets absorbed into a larger megalopolis or not. One distinction I'm making there is that we might effectively have a megalopolis, but we don't actually give it a name. It's still just going to be called a city, even though it's right up against other cities. Functionally speaking, they may form a megalopolis, but no one's probably going to call it that. Lastly, another word for megalopolis is metropolis.

IN SPACE

Let's talk about settlements in space. There's what I'm calling a "vacuum settlement." This means any settlement that is surrounded by a vacuum instead of breathable air. This reality will completely dominate how life is in that settlement. Since such a settlement doesn't happen naturally, we are completely fabricating how that is laid out. We can pretty much do whatever we want – within reason, of course. These can range in size from a village to a city, and many of the issues we've talked about will apply to these.

Naturally, one of the most important aspects of such a place is that no one interferes with the oxygen supply. This could literally kill everyone. And, as you might imagine, there's probably going to be significant technology preventing such a thing from happening. This means not only redundant systems, but significant military who are protecting these. Such a place is likely to have significant rules for even something as simple as opening a door from one place to another could lead to depressurization.

As you can imagine, most people living there probably have a significant understanding of the risks. They almost certainly have an interest in certain kinds of laws being obeyed; those laws being the ones about that kind of interference. Even someone who considers themselves a rebel is unlikely to be willing to go that far with their rebelliousness that they interfere with such a thing. Visitors might also be closely watched and monitored to make sure that their access to one thing or another is tightly controlled.

WHAT'S NOT COVERED

Now, before we wrap up with how to start creating a settlement, I want to talk about a few things that are not going to be included in this episode. These are additional subjects that are included in *Creating Places* in Chapter 6.

One of these is the defense and offense of such places, such as the fortifications like archery towers, cleared areas, castles and, of course, the wall. There's also a discussion of what kind of armed forces are really located here, from the local guards to cavalry, knights, flying forces and beyond. Then there's the importance of how our settlement is known to others, and from within its own population. This includes not only reputation, but its colors, symbols, slogans and even the products that they produce. All of these can make our settlements more interesting and believable.

WHERE TO START

Finally, let's talk about where to start with inventing a settlement. It's a good idea to start with a settlement's location because this is going to affect so many things about it. This includes not only its layout, but the climate and, therefore, how people dress, for example, and even the plant life and animals that are nearby. The neighbors are also important to decide soon, and this includes things like the terrain, such as a forest or mountain because that's going to impact how easy it is to reach this place and what products and livelihood they can create for themselves.

We should also determine where it is within a sovereign power, such as how close to the border or further in because that's also going to impact the fortifications. The most important of these neighbors is, arguably, any neighbor that affects the number of species and kind of species that are located here. The size and population is a major area to consider after you've decided where this settlement is located. This will determine much about what life is like here, including the society's worldview. The smaller areas that we can worry about later are things like its reputation, how well it is known and things like the symbols and slogans. These are not things that are going to have a major impact on our use of this place, but just add some color and depth.

And, as with everything with world building, the most important thing is to start with something where you have a solid idea. As long as you've got one, just go with it and it doesn't really matter what order you do these things in. It's just really a question of whether you have an idea or not. And if you don't, then I recommend doing the order we've talked about here. But if you have an idea, go ahead and work on that first, exhaust it, do what you can, invent everything you can think of and then worry about some of these other things.

TRAVEL OVER LAND

Hello and welcome to *The Art of World Building Podcast*, episode number sixteen. Today's topic talks about how to determine travel times for horses, wagons, people and more through various kinds of terrains and what can slow us down, and how. This material and more is discussed in chapter 7 of *Creating Places*, volume 2 in *The Art of World Building* book series.

GENERAL TIPS

Now, in the intro, I mentioned that we are talking about a fantasy setting here, but really, any setting where we don't have modern technology will do because we're going to be talking about things like walking, being in a wagon and riding horses that are encumbered to one degree or another by supplies and armor – armor for the horse and knights who are wearing full plate armor, for example. In a typical science fiction setting, we're not going to have that problem because people are going to be using machines to get somewhere. If people are using machines like those that we have here on Earth, then you don't really need me to explain how fast a car goes because we all know that. If you have invented a technology, well then, you can pretty much invent how fast that's actually going to go and therefore, again, I can't really second guess what speeds you're going to decide on. So, that's something that you can basically invent and not have to worry about being realistic. Maybe I shouldn't put it that way, but what I mean is that no one can call you on it and tell you that your imaginary engine that only exists in your setting goes a different speed because they can't say that. You're the one who created it, therefore you are the one who decides how this actually works.

In that sense, you're kind of on your own. I don't mean to abandon you there, but it's actually kind of a good thing because you can make this up and not worry about it too much. On the other hand, if you've got a fantasy setting or another kind of setting where we don't have even modern technology, there are things like horses and wagons, and we should know how fast people can actually go on these. In your science fiction setting, you might still need to understand the stuff that's in this particular episode because even though your characters might have faster ways of getting around, like a ship, that ship can always crash or break down and, as a result, your characters might be reduced to walking, using a wagon, a horse or similar animal of your own invention.

Now, some of us may not need to worry about this anyway because if we don't have a map that we're going to release with our story, and if we don't intend on doing a lot of stories there, then we may not need to worry about this too much. But it kind of depends on what you say. If you say that it is 250 miles between one place and another and your characters are going to get there by walking, and they're going to do that in 2 days, that's not going to happen. A simple way around this problem is to not tell people how many miles or kilometers it is from one place to another. You could do the opposite and tell people how many miles it is, but not tell them how long it takes to get there, but that's not something that we usually want to do in a story. People want to know how long it's going to take. Not because they care about how long the journey's actually going to be, but because the characters are going to be going a certain number of days and we're probably going to be showing a certain amount of that travel time.

So, if we have a choice between not mentioning the distance or not mentioning the time frame, the distance is the one we're not going to mention. Now, if we want to be a little more accurate and give people some more sense of realism or that we know what we're talking about, then we want to start thinking about the combination of them and acknowledging both of those and being accurate. And by being accurate, I don't mean exactly 26 hours to walk from one place to another. We want to be within a range such as 22 to maybe 28 hours. One of the ways we can use that kind of range is we might want to just suggest that the characters can make it in a leisurely fashion or they might have to really hurry to get there. If we have some understanding of how long it might really take, we can get an understanding of which way we might want to spin that. In other words, this can help us characterize the journey.

If we understand that it could take 22 to 28 hours to get there, depending on circumstances, and we need them to get there in 22 hours, then we can characterize this as them being in a hurry and they just need to get on with this. Most of us have some difficulty understanding what's realistic, and that's the goal of this podcast episode and the corresponding chapter of the *Creating Places* book.

On that note, I am going to admit there is a lot of detail in charts that I have in the book that I'm not going to cover in this podcast just because it's kind of hard to describe charts of information. But I'm still going to give you the explanations and give you the understanding of how these things work, and maybe by the end we'll go through at least one of these charts so you'll see how it can be applied.

Another note I'm going to make here is that most of the Earth uses the metric system, but I'm going to just talk in miles mostly because that's what I'm more familiar with and I'm here in the United States. If you pick up a copy of *Creating Places*, I do have the calculations in both measurements. And one of the things about it is that the amount of time it takes to go doesn't change. It's really just which set of numbers you're using. Understanding the principles is universal. For those of you who do have a map, I would also recommend writing the words "not drawn to scale" on that map just because that gives us a little bit of leeway.

Despite that, when I do a map, even if I put those words on there, I actually intend it to be to scale because I'm going to go ahead and measure stuff and figure out, "Okay, one inch equals twenty-five miles in my world," and then I'm going to use that as a way of figuring out the relative distances, but I don't necessarily tell my audience that just because there's always going to be that guy who's a smart ass who comes along saying, "Well, you know, I've looked and this is not that distance," or whatever. So, just to avoid that kind of bologna, I sometimes want to put "not drawn to scale" on my maps.

TRAVEL MODES

The first mode of travel I'm going to talk about is one that's available to most of us, and that is walking. The basic problem with walking is how long it takes to get from one place to another, and the fact that you're going to have to carry anything you want to take with you. These days, it's so much easier to bring a lot of luggage, but back in the day on Earth, people traveled pretty light – if they traveled at all.

And most of that traveling was done by foot to places that were in a relatively short distance of each other. It was fairly common for people to have never traveled outside a small range. This is something that is arguably overlooked in fantasy because most people just don't have that big of an understanding about what the rest of the world is like, and of course, information in such a setting doesn't travel nearly as well or accurately as it does today.

What I'm getting at there is that there's a tremendous amount of ignorance about what's really going on in the rest of the world, and reliance upon just rumors and what people are saying. And who knows how often people are accurate? Another thing to keep in mind is that people have to be relatively healthy to make such a journey. Most of the people who were doing such traveling were going to be, probably, between the ages of 10 and 40, given that the lifespan wasn't particularly long back then and, in fact, 40 could be considered rather old to be doing such a thing.

You will have to decide what the fitness level is for the people in your world and how much getting around by foot they really do. I would recommend making a kind of general note in your world building file for this particular setting, just saying that people don't travel outside 100 miles very often, and when they travel, they generally do so by foot. In such a setting, someone could reasonably claim to have traveled really far and wide without actually having gone terribly far. They could say they've been to the other side of the world when they have never gone more than 500 miles away, but even that amount of knowledge is so far in excess of what other people have.

This seems like a good opportunity for someone who's a skilled liar to acquire a reputation for having traveled farther and to places where they never have been, and then, next thing they know, someone like the king has said, "Hey, I understand you've been to this kingdom so far away. We need someone who understands that place and who's been there, so we're going to send you." And that person is realizing, "Oops, I don't actually know that place. I lied, but I can't admit it." So, you know, this is something we can do with our stories.

So, we're talking about walking – and I do mean walking. Most people are not going to run any measurable distance on a journey unless they are trained warriors or messengers. It's just not realistic and, of course, it's kind of hard to run when you're carrying something like a big backpack on your back. So, that's also going to be a problem. If you were to create a chart of how long it takes to walk between two locations and how long it takes to run between two locations, well, I wouldn't actually create that column that says running because they're not going to be able to do that for very long. I would just assume that someone who is trained to do that kind of thing would be able to do it in maybe a few hours less. Again, we need ballparks here, not dead-on accuracy.

OBSTACLES

Typically, in our stories, we don't want travel between two locations to be terribly easy. What I'm thinking of here is things like monsters or nasty species who are out there and who could attack our characters. This could certainly impact our travel time if we are afraid of attracting the attention of any such thing, and we are therefore trying to move quietly. It might also mean that we have to hide for prolonged periods of time. It also likely means that our characters will have weapons. It might not be all of our characters. The typical adventuring party, yes. We're going to have weapons. But if it's someone like a merchant who needs to get from one place to another to do business, not necessarily bringing a wagon of supplies with him, but just maybe going to meet someone that he wants to arrange a business deal with, he may not have weapons, or be good at them, so, of course, he may hire someone to accompany him. But not everyone's going to have a weapon.

Bear in mind that some places are obviously safer or more dangerous than others. In addition, we might have formal messengers who are acting on the behalf of a king, for example, and we may decide for whatever reason that we have a law where those messengers cannot be molested in any way. And, therefore, they may not actually have a whole lot of weapons with them if that law is reasonably followed. If it's not followed, then of course they will have it, but that's going to cause other problems if no one's really enforcing that law. But I'm just tossing this out as something else to consider. We may have messengers who are able to go without wearing a lot of armor or carrying a lot of weapons because the area's relatively safe and most people do not interfere with them. These are all factors that can speed up or hinder their ability to travel quickly.

Something else to consider is that in a fantasy setting, or something similar, we often have imaginary species like elves. Well, the elves are roughly the same height as humans, so their ability to travel is not going to be hugely impacted and different from ours just because they might be six inches taller. On the other hand, dwarves are quite a bit shorter than us and their ability to travel quickly might be impacted. It will literally take them more steps to make the same journey. This could not only slow them, but it could have an endurance issue where they just can't travel as far in a single day.

Whether we use these species or we invent our own, we should pay a little bit of attention to this. Maybe we have a group of four humans who could make the journey in 20 hours, but they've got a dwarf with them. Due to this, it could take them 25 hours. And some of them might be chaffing about this as they're traveling. Either they are constantly giving the dwarf grief that he needs to hurry up, or the dwarf needs to take breaks more often and the others feel fine and they don't want to deal with this.

If you're creating a chart of travel times, you may want to have a column for humans versus another species. If everyone is to stick together, the entire group must move at the pace of the slowest person. There is a way around this. We could decide that the dwarves might take longer to make the trip, but they have more endurance and, therefore, they can actually walk longer. If a human would be exhausted in eight hours, well, the dwarf might be able to go ten hours. Since the humans are forced to walk a little bit slower, they might also be able to go ten hours.

So, let's talk some numbers. How far can the typical human walk reliably, day after day, without needing to rest or be exhausted after they're done? The answer is 12 miles. We can obviously do more than that in a single day, but we might be exhausted. In fact, we could do so much in a single day that we might be bedridden for a few days after that. So, we do have some leeway here, but we should be aware of the impact that this is going to have on our character if they go beyond that. A Roman legion back in the day could do 14 to 20 miles per day, but they were trained to do this. The average human could do 20 miles a day, but they're going to be exhausted. Keep these numbers in mind. They're going to be very useful to you.

Let's switch gears to riding a horse. Now, you may have another form of animal that's very similar to that, but we're just going to talk about horses because that's what we have here on Earth. Actually, there are other animals, like the donkey or the elephant, but the same principles are going to apply. And if we've invented something, it's going to be similar in that it has a base number of miles per day that it can reasonably travel.

So, with a horse or another animal, we have three basic levels of encumbrance, which is basically light, medium, and heavy. What I mean by encumbrance is how much stuff that horse is actually carrying. As you would imagine, the more you're carrying, the more it's going to slow you down and the more it's going to wear on you and reduce your endurance. That, in turn, is going to affect how many miles a day you can actually travel. This is one reason you might see a traveler portrayed as having a horse with them, but the horse is a pack animal that is carrying all their luggage, basically, and the human is still walking.

For minimal gear, such as spare clothes, a sword, some utensils and some water, this is going to be the lightest load and the person who can travel the farthest in a day on a horse. With a horse, that's going to be roughly 30 to 40 miles. We're talking about 30 to 40 miles, day after day, without that horse needing to rest. By contrast, we may have a fully armored knight who is wearing plate armor and has multiple swords, maybe a lance, and it might be a warhorse that he's riding where that warhorse is also fully armored with plate armor. This is, actually, one reason you might see such a horse not having that much stuff on them when there's no battle that's expected, and there is a secondary horse that is being used as a pack animal, where that horse is lugging around all this stuff so that the warhorse is fresh and gets suited up in time for the actual fight. In any case, such a warhorse that is fully armored like that, and is carrying someone else who is also fully armored, is going to have far less endurance and speed.

Then there's the middle ground between these, and that might be someone who is only wearing chainmail, a shield, and maybe just one sword. And if the horse is armored, it might just be wearing leather.

There are specialized horses that can go over 100 miles per day for several days in a row, and the Pony Express in the US is one such version of this. However, such a horse was basically incapable of doing much of anything for several days after that. When these riders would reach the next station, they would trade that horse in for a fresh one so that they could continue going at the breakneck speed.

If we're using horses to pull a wagon, the wagon can travel between 15 to 25 miles per day when there are no roads. If we want to slow them down, we can just have the wagon get stuck in mud, for example. Roads tend to spend things up, but we may be talking about dirt roads because cobblestones can actually be really brutal on the entire structure of a wagon, causing things to kind of rattle loose.

FLYING

The last mode of travel that we're going to talk about is flying. We tend to assume that anything flying is going to do so in a straight line, and we even have an expression that something is, say, 20 miles "as straight as the crow flies." Well, I can tell you that if that crow has to go over a mountain, it's not going to go in a straight line. It's probably going to go around the mountain. This will depend on how tall that mountain is. Even real birds struggle to climb over the Himalayas because those are so tall. We have a tendency to depict dragons as being all-powerful, but one way to make them a little more realistic is that they might also have trouble getting over mountains. And, in fact, that's probably true. If you ignore the impossibility of dragons flying at all, because they're so big and so heavy, we could still make them have trouble getting over these mountains just because they are so heavy. There's not that much air. It's thinner air. It's going to be that much harder for their wings to propel them over them. A dragon being forced to go around is can make them more realistic.

If we don't like that idea and we want some sort of explanation for how they can just easily go over really tall mountains, we can just decide that they are magical beings and that this aids them in doing so. We may or may not want to explain that to people because some people don't really like it when there's an explanation for something. Or, at least, they don't like it when we explain something implausible. By the way, you may remember from a previous episode that the tallest mountains are those that are on the interior of the continent rather than at the coast.

A hostile territory can also change the flight pattern. Let's say that dragons are rideable and that two adjacent kingdoms have people who can ride those dragons, and those two kingdoms are hostile to each other. The people in one of those kingdoms might want to fly around the other one rather than over it to get to a destination on the other side. A lone dragon may be afraid to fly through an area that is inhabited by many other dragons, especially if those other dragons are hostile or territorial. As I say that, it occurs to me that most people seem to want to portray dragons as being fearless, but that's not realistic either.

Now, on Earth, all animals that are capable of carrying a rider are imaginary, but none of them would be affected by the terrain except for these really tall mountains, so they could fly right over roads, forests, rolling hills or deserts without really being impacted by these. If there are nasty things living in a forest, well, this flying animal could just go right over it, at least if it's going high enough.

UNDERSTAND TRAVEL BY FLIGHT

When we're trying to figure out how far an invented animal could travel in a day, it's a good idea to understand how a real Earth animal can do so and start from there. A carrier pigeon goes about 50 miles an hour and can cover up to 700 miles in a day. A hawk can go about 20 to 40 miles an hour during migration. We don't really care how fast they're going when they're diving down at prey because that's not a travel concern, and that's what we're focusing on here.

If we have invented a humanoid species that has wings, bear in mind that it's not going to be nearly as aerodynamic as a bird. The same is really true of a dragon. Some of them are shown as having four giant legs, not to mention that giant body. This is not really an aerodynamic shape compared to a bird. Without magic, not only is something shaped like a bird going to be faster, but it's going to have more maneuverability in the air.

And that brings us to something that has almost no maneuverability in the air, and that's the airship. Now, these are also known by other names like blimps and dirigibles. Some of these might actually exist in a fantasy setting, and they could certainly do so in a science fiction one. We could decide that magic is powering such a vessel to some degree. A large airship like the Hindenburg had a high speed of 84 miles an hour, but 70 mph was the maximum speed for the smaller ones and most of them typically cruised between 30 and 50 miles per hour. In other words, that cruising speed is what we're typically going to use.

The largest of these could fly as high as 24,000 feet, which means they are, theoretically, able to fly over any mountain range on Earth. However, in reality, they didn't typically go that high and that would also cause problems such as the payload could reduce how high they can go.

Most of them tended to operate mainly between something like 1,500 and 8,000 feet. Passenger ships were typically for sightseeing and, therefore, they flew much lower, such as under 650 feet. These can typically fly in a straight line, and most of them had a duration of about 24 to 50 hours, but the Hindenburg could actually fly over 100 hours, although that was typically only done when they were crossing an ocean.

By contrast, there is the balloon which just drifts with the wind. They cannot be propelled through the air, and they cannot control their flight path. Or, I should say, they have very limited ability to control the flight path. They also go pretty slow, averaging somewhere between three to six miles per hour. Then, of course, there's the airplane, but I'm not going to cover that in this episode anymore than I did so in the book because the variety of planes is so extreme that trying to summarize them would not serve a world builder well.

THE IMPACT OF TERRAIN

We've already talked a little bit about obstacles that terrain can cause, but I want to touch on this a little bit more. If our characters need to travel through a forest, then there is an assumption that this forest could slow them down depending on how thick the underbrush is. This makes perfect sense, but one thing that we should consider is that there may be roads through that forest. If there are, then it doesn't really matter how much underbrush is off to the side of that road because the road itself is mostly clear, unless something like a tree has fallen down over the path and we have wagons.

In a previous episode, we talked about different kinds of forests, such as a savanna, a woodland or just your regular, old, run of the mill forest. Each one of these has a different density of underbrush. There's a good reason to decide on what each forest is like before deciding on how hard it is to travel through it. On the other hand, something like rolling hills, foothills, and certainly mountains are going to slow everyone, regardless of whether there's a road or not because you still have to go up and down. Even so, a road could help if it is in decent condition just because it'll give a smoother surface that is more uniform and less unpredictable.

Now, when it comes to road, they are not like what we have in our modern times when we have asphalt, which is pretty smooth. In a fantasy setting in particular, we are more likely talking about cobblestones or a trail where the road is basically hardpacked earth. Unless it rains, a dirt road can be fairly reliable. However, there is always the issue of wear and tear on such a road because one area of it is going to be more worn down than another, and we're not talking about an entire mile so much as every 10 feet there could be part of the road that is more depressed and, as a result, water has collected there and there's more mud. Generally, it's an unpredictable ride.

Horses also do not prefer hard asphalt or cobblestones. They would rather be walking on hardpacked earth. It's preferable if there is a certain amount of grass there as well. The reason I mention this is that when we're trying to figure out how long it would take for someone to get somewhere, or how much endurance they have, if there is an actual cobblestone road, and we're talking about horses, they may not actually want to be on the road. The riders probably know that maybe they should be off to one side of the road.

So, even if there is a road, maybe it's not being used because the riders are smarter than that. Any cobblestones, also, are not going to extend very far from a settlement just because it's very expensive to create these. If you're drawing a map of your world and you're using lines to indicate where the roads are, you may want to use a solid line where there is a road, and then a dashed line where it's only going to be a trail.

By trail, I mean something that's not paved. Generally, you would only draw that dashed line a short distance, less than 10 miles from the actual settlement. And we're really only talking cities or the larger towns that are even going to have these roads. Note that I'm really talking about roads that are outside the settlement. Inside the settlement, you might have more cobblestones. I haven't mentioned this before because we've really been talking about travel between two destinations.

TRAVEL TIMES

Now, as I mentioned earlier, there is an entire chapter about travel over land in the *Creating Places* book, and there are a significant number of charts and calculations in there to figure out how long it takes to get from one place to another. What I did there is a typical setup for a fantasy world, so I did something like a riding horse, a lightly encumbered horse and then a heavy war horse, wagons, dragons, things like carrier pigeons and, of course, humans for walking. For each of these, I did some research on what the average travel time is, day after day, without being so fatigued that you can't go any further the day after that. I used the term "base miles per day," even if you're talking about kilometers, to refer to this number.

What we want to do is have that number and then modify that based on terrain. I forget the numbers off the top of my head, but for humans it was base miles per day of 12, and then I would modify that by a number based on roads or heavy forest with no road through that forest, or rolling hills, to see how many miles per day you would actually travel based on that condition changing it. This allows me to approximate how long it might take. Now, in my main world that I've been building for 30 years called Llurien, I also calculated for the maps that 1 inch is something like 25 miles, therefore 2 inches is 50 miles and so on. I measured the distance between various locations so I have that information.

Using a spreadsheet I have, I can then calculate how long it takes to get from one place to another based on the terrain. When writing the *Creating Places* book, I took that spreadsheet and modified it, removing my information from my world and putting in some sample data. I give this spreadsheet away for free to anyone who joins the newsletter. What this means is that you can do the same thing with your setting. You can measure the distance between two places and input some numbers, and the spreadsheet will calculate for you how long it will take to get there by various modes of locomotion based on the terrain.

Now, some of that has a lot of work to it, and if I had it to do over again, I don't know that I would, so there's another tab on that spreadsheet where it's a little bit more generic. What I mean is that instead of having every two points on my map laid out and how long that takes, I just have a kind of general chart that says, "Okay, this number of miles will take this long to do." The advantage of that chart is that you don't have to do any calculations at all, and not even really any measuring. You can just eyeball your map. Or, if you don't have a map, just decide, "Okay, it's 55 miles between these two places, and the chart says that would take this number of miles if you are traveling by this way." And then you could add or subtract slightly from that if you don't agree with my modifiers.

Basically, what I'm telling you is that a lot of this work has already been done for you and you can get it for free. If you really want to understand the nuts and bolts of how all of that works, you can buy the *Creating Places* book and there is quite a bit of stuff in Chapter 7, I believe, about how all of that works and what my thinking is on all of it.

TRAVEL OVER WATER

Hello and welcome to *The Art of World Building Podcast*, episode number seventeen. Today's topic is about how travel over water is impacted by wind, ship types, and more. Learn how to determine travel times over water when using oars or the wind. This includes ship types like the frigate, galley, ship-of-the-line, and more. This material and more is discussed in chapter 8 of *Creating Places*, volume 2 in *The Art of World Building* series.

GENERAL TIPS

This is another episode that may apply more to fantasy world builders than science fiction ones, simply because, in science fiction, most of the travel is done through the air — or the absence of air in space. However, our science fiction characters could end up having to travel by water if they crash land on a planet and there's no other way of getting around. I'm also talking about traveling by wind power or by oars, not by engines.

In science fiction, we could either invent the kind of engines that people have and how fast that means they can go, or we can base things on engines here on Earth. One reason I'm not going to cover that is that engines are significantly more predictable than the wind. This is not to say that sea conditions cannot affect how fast someone is going because, of course, they can, but I am admittedly targeting those who write fantasy, or a setting that does not have that kind of technology.

Now, most of us have no idea how long it takes to get from one place to another by various kinds of ships, or how fast those ships can travel, or anything about how these ships really work. Watching something like *The Pirates of the Caribbean* movies, it doesn't really help you understand this. If anything, it gives you the impression of not understanding this at all, which is how I always felt.

Now, there are a number of things that impact the difficulty of sailing between two different locations, and one of those is the wind. The direction of this can change and, also, the strength of that wind can change. Some countries are also better at building ships that are more seaworthy, and they also might have better sailors and therefore a better navy. All of this influences the trade routes that are going to show up, which nations can conquer others, or how difficult it is for them to do so.

Using the wind, we have a lot of leeway for how long it might actually take someone to get from one place to another. Depending on your point of view, this can either be good or bad. The good part is if our calculations are not exact, well, it's not going to be exact anyway, so that's just something that comes with the territory. The bad part is we don't have a fixed answer that we can use and we have to do a certain amount of guesswork. Unless, of course, you understand the contents of this podcast episode, or the corresponding chapter of the *Creating Places* book, which has some charts that really help with this.

There are several reasons why we have this leeway, and one of those is that if we have drawn a map, we should just write on there that it is not drawn to scale. If we have oarsmen, they are not going to be able to row at the same speed indefinitely, and their endurance and training is going to change from ship to ship. So, one crew might be able to go faster than another. Of course, wind speed is not consistent, and then the wind direction is also not consistent. Both of these can affect the speed. Different types of ships also sail at different speeds under the same exact conditions. If you have a frigate that is chasing a ship-of-the-line, it might be faster. Another thing to bear in mind is that ships are weighed down by the people who are on there. Some of those can be killed in combat, for example, and then there's the cargo, the amount of food and, of course, the weapons and ammunition.

At the start of, let's say, a five-month journey, the ship is going to be weighed down more than at the end. So, in theory, it's going to be traveling slower. The ship can, of course, be damaged. My favorite explanation for why we have leeway is that our ship might be sailing on a fictitious planet with, possibly, a different number of moons and anything else that may affect the seas. This could be a kind of cheap excuse if we say that a frigate is sailing a certain number of nautical miles at a certain speed and, therefore, it reaches its destination in a certain number of days, and someone on Earth says, "Well, that's not possible," and we say, "Hey, man. This is a fictional planet. You can't really say that. I'm the god of this place. I say what really works here and what goes."

So, that could be considered a cop out, and the information in this podcast and the corresponding chapter is going to help you not have to resort to that explanation. Of course, not having a sailor call us out on what we've said is one reason for this, but we just might want to be more accurate and we can use the information that we learn for characterizing the journey that people are taking.

For example, maybe we have learned that it'll take our characters, traveling on a certain type of ship in certain conditions, 20 hours to get somewhere, but we need them to take 25 hours. So, what do we do? Well, maybe we throw up a storm. Maybe that storm damages one of the masts. So, this can cause us to think of things that we can put into our story so it's not just an easy trip that is glossed over and not even mentioned. Of course, we could do that kind of thing anyway without having to throw out any numbers, but you get the idea.

SHIP TERMS

Let's cover a few ship terms so that we all are talking the same language. The only ones I'm going to cover here are the ones you need to understand in order to understand the difference between one type of ship and another because we're going to be talking about that more later.

The mast is the vertical pole you see in the middle of the ship. Some ships have none, some only have one, some have two and some of them have three. In a few cases, there are actually four of these. Technically, there's even a ship with five, which I believe is called a clipper ship, but we're not going to really be worrying about that one.

There are other terms, like the center mast is obviously the one in the middle, the foremast is the one at the front of the ship and the one at the back is often called the mizzenmast. But we'll just call that the rear mast to keep this easier. That mast is usually the shortest. The one in the middle is usually the tallest. If a ship only has two masts, the one in the back is the one that's usually not there.

What's the point of a mast? Well, it's to hold the yards. Those are the horizontal bars that the sails are actually attached to. Now, as it turns out, not all of the yards are horizontal, but most of them are. There's also an expression you may have heard, and that is that a ship is square rigged. What this means is that if the ship is headed north to south and the yards are east to west, they are squared up with each other. That's what a square-rigged ship means.

On the other hand, there's something known as lateen-rigged ships. That means that the yard is sloped and runs parallel to the ship. So, if the ship is pointing north/south, the yard is also pointing north/south.

Most ships have anywhere from one to three yards per mast, and there are names for these yards, but we don't need to know what they are in order to understand what we're talking about here today. Some ships actually have a combination of the square and lateen rigging, and what that typically means is that the main mast and the front foremast are square rigged, and the mizzenmast, or the rear mast, is lateen rigged. The reason I'm mentioning this is that some of this is going to come up when we talk about the different types of ships because the rigging is one way to identify them. As you might imagine, the number of yards, sails and the way they're configured have an affect on the ship's speed.

Lastly, we want to talk about the sails. In a square-rigged ship, the sails are actually in the shape of a trapezoid, which means that they're wider at the bottom than they are at the top where they are attached to the yard. On the lateen-rigged ships, the sail is usually triangular. And if you're having trouble picture that, just picture a sailboat. On the other hand, in the movies like *The Pirates of the Caribbean*, the square-rigged ships are what you see. One way that this affects the ship speeds is that the square-rigged ships do pretty well in the open ocean because the wind speed is usually fairly constant, or at least it is more so than it is closer to shore. The direction is also fairly constant, again, as it compares to being closer to shore.

When you are closer to shore, the lateen rigging allows the sailors to change the sail more quickly to take advantage of the wind speed direction. This greater adjustment ability allows for better maneuverability and can make the lateen-rigged ships sail faster when they're closer to shore compared to a ship that is exclusively square-rigged. Next, we're going to talk about ship rates.

SHIP RATES

It's time to talk about ship rates. I don't mean, "Hey, that's a first-rate ship, or a third-rate ship," in the sense that first-rate is a really good ship and third-rate is kind of a mediocre one. That's not what we mean by ship rates. The ratings are not a judgment of quality. It's really just about the number of guns and personnel. We're going to talk about this later, but we may not want guns and gunpowder, and therefore cannons, on our world, and we might want to have to replace those with something that is plausible. But, for the sake of this conversation about ship rates, we're just going to talk about what the British Navy does. And, of course, they have cannons. So, that's what we're going to be talking about.

I've got a handy little chart that I'm going to gloss over kind of quickly here, but it basically includes the officers, seamen and boys, and servants in the count of the men who are aboard. A first-rate ship is going to have somewhere between 100 and 112 guns, and 841 men. These are the biggest ships. By contrast, a sixth-rated ship, which is the lowest, is going to have somewhere between 20 and 28 guns, and 128 to 198 men. Now, in between those two extremes, we have the second-, third-, fourth- and fifth-rate ships, but I'm not going to throw out a bunch of numbers for you because it's probably not going to stick.

Anything that had fewer than 20 guns, which is the sixth-rate ship, was not considered a rated ship. All of the ships that we just mentioned, the sixth-rate through the first-rate, had three masts. Now, the two biggest classes, the first- and second-rate ships, had three full decks just for the guns, which is a lot of firepower. That means they were carrying as few as 90 guns and as many as 112 guns.

Now, the third- and fourth-rate ships had two gundecks, and the fifth- and sixth-rated ships only had one gundeck. So, the first and second have three decks, the third and fourth have two decks, and the fifth- and sixth-rated ships have one deck. Well, these are the decks devoted to only guns. For any ship that had more than one gundeck, the biggest guns were on the bottom because you don't want them on the top because that would make the ship top-heavy and more likely to turn over.

Ship Types

Now, we're going to start talking about the ship types, which is where this stuff gets interesting. As world builders, we could invent our own ship types, but I don't think we really need to because people are not sick of the ones that already exist. One reason for that is, possibly, that ships are not typically shown in any sort of great detail, even if they do appear in a fantasy book. By contrast, if seemingly every fantasy book has elves in it, for example, and therefore people get kind of over exposed to this, some people might just think that they want to see something new. I don't think the same thing happens with wooden ships.

So, with that in mind, when we're talking about ship types, we're going to look at some of the most prominent kinds that were around on Earth. This is less about inventing ships than using existing ones and understanding what we're talking about. Now, vessels come in two basic groups: The long ships and the round ships. Now, the round ships are not actually circular, of course, but they are called that because they are wide when compared to the narrow and streamlined long ships like those that the Vikings used. And, as it turns out, we're only going to talk about one long ship, and that's called the galley.

The long ships are the earliest types of ships, and all of them were basically designed for war or really fast transportation, not carrying cargo. They were usually powered by oars, but they would have maybe one sail for additional propulsion at times. The galley is the ship that is synonymous with Vikings, although it was used elsewhere. It usually had a single mast for that sail, and it had a metal prow at the front so that it could ram another boat and board it. While it's a really maneuverable ship, it has a really wide turning arch and it requires calm weather. While it can be used to go on the open seas, it wasn't typically used that way. It was mostly found along the shoreline.

The invention of guns and the addition of cannons to bigger ships is one of the reasons why this kind of ship fell out of favor. So, if your world doesn't have that kind of firepower, the galley might be one of the more commonly seen vessels. Some of these could be quite large and have a forecastle and a rear castle for artillery and soldiers, and as many as 25 oars on either side, each oar being rowed by 5 men. However, this is not the kind of ship that's being used for war. If it is being used in war, it's leading the vanguard. This is where the captain of a fleet of galleys would be.

The presence of the forecastle and the rear castle means that the captain and whoever else can go and have a private conversation – or relatively private conversation. As you can imagine, that has some advantages.

Round Ships

It's time to talk about the round ships. We have quite a few that we're going to discuss. The round ships were originally designed for carrying cargo and passengers. But, of course, they have been used for war. This is pretty much what you've seen in every pirate movie. Unless I say otherwise, all of the ships we're going to talk about are square-rigged on all of the masts. Now, you may have heard the term "man-of-war," but this is not an actual ship type. It's just a generic English name for any three-masted warship that has soldiers and cannons. Two examples of a man-of-war are the frigate and ship-of-the-line, but those are, of course, two different ship types.

Now, I have a chart that, this time, lists out the different ship types and how many guns they have, how many crew, the maximum speed in knots, and their total length. And, of course, the name of each ship. I suggest going onto www.artofworldbuilding.com and looking for the *Creating Places* book in the menu. You can find a link that says "images." This image of the chart is available online for free.

The ships we're going to look at are the brig, frigate, galleon, gunboat, ship-of-the-line, sloop and sloop-of-war. Fortunately, all of them have a maximum speed of 11 knots. The frigate and the gunboat can go up to 14 knots.

By the way, I also have a picture of each ship type that we're going to talk about, which is also available online.

First, we're going to talk about the brig, which is a two-masted, square-rigged ship that has a single gundeck. This ship is really fast, highly maneuverable and it can be used as a merchant ship, warship or a scouting vessel. Pirates really like these because all of these.

The frigate is also fast and highly maneuverable, and is a fourth or fifth-rated ship with one gundeck. These are often used as scouting vessels for a fleet, escorting something, patrolling or acting independently. In fact, these are the largest ships that worked independently because the bigger ships were considered too valuable to risk being captured or destroyed. This is something that's more likely to happen if a ship is traveling alone. Now, there is something known as a heavy frigate, and that means a frigate that has two gundecks instead of only one. They are the same length as bigger ships, like the ships-of-the-line, but they have so little firepower by comparison that they would typically just run away from such a vessel. Otherwise, they would quite literally get blown out of the water.

We'll talk more about ships-of-the-line in a minute, but during a line of battle where there's a row of ships on one side, and then the enemy's also got a row of ships on the other, the frigates were not part of that ship-of-the-line configuration. That's why they're not called one. The frigates were present, but they were typically behind the line. The reason they were there is that they would relay signals from one ship to another. Imagine if you're the last ship in a ship-of-the-line. All you can see is the ship in front of you. You can't communicate to anything that's farther along. Therefore, you would communicate to a frigate which was off to one side, and that frigate would relay signals farther up the line. The rules of engagement also dictated that these ships were not actually fired upon unless the frigate had fired upon another ship first.

Let's talk about the fireship, which is an interesting variation. This is not a type of ship because any ship can be turned into a fireship. This kind of ship is designed to be set on fire and then sent into the enemy line of ships to, hopefully, catch other ships on fire. This obviously means certain destruction to itself, and therefore valuable ships like the ships-of-the-line were not used for such a vessel.

Another ship type is the galleon, which has two features that distinguish it from other ship types. That is the mast and the prow at the front of the ship. The prow just has a distinguishable look to it that you would recognize if you saw a picture of one. Another way to spot this ship is that the center mast and the foremast at the front are square-rigged like all of these round ships that we're talking about, but the mizzenmast, the one at the rear, is latten-rigged instead. That allows for a better point of sailing. As a result, this galleon could actually save days or even weeks on a long voyage over the open ocean. In other words, it would leave behind other ship types.

Then there's the gunboat, which we may have to rename if we don't have guns in our world. But this boat is really small and it usually only has one or two cannons on it. It's designed to be used in coastal waters and take on large ships where it's easily outmatched, but if you have a dozen of these, they can do horrific damage to a larger ship just by surrounding it and blowing holes in it. These are cheap and easily replaced.

On the opposite extreme is the ship-of-the-line. This is a ship with at least 60 guns. This includes all first-, second-, and third-rate ships. They get their name because of this configuration where they sail in a straight line, firing at a parallel line of enemy ships. The reason both sides do this is so that they don't accidentally hit their own ships. The first-rate ships-of-the-line are the biggest ships on the sea.

On the opposite extreme is the sloop, which for most of us means a sailboat. This is too small to be a ship of war, and it's only something we're going to use if our characters need a small, wind-powered vessel to get from one place to another. If we would like them to use oars instead of a sail and the wind, then we might have them use the galley, which was the long ship that we talked about first.

Now, the sloop is not to be confused with the sloop-of-war, which also is called a corvette, kind of like the car. As the name implies, this is a warship that has a single gundeck with 18 guns. These are not rated ships because they only have 18 guns and that does not meet the minimum of 20 in the British system. But, of course, we can invent our own system and maybe call these seventh-rate ships. The sloop-of-war has all sorts of different sail configurations, not just the square-rigged one.

The last one we're going to talk about is the privateer, but this is not really a ship type. Any ship that is operated by a private individual, or a group of them, for profit is considered a privateer. A sovereign power would give something known as a "letter of marque" to the captain of the ship, and that authorized this captain to engage in acts of war against other ships. Any time it got the loot from this, a certain percentage of that captured prize was supposed to go to the sovereign power. If you're thinking this sounds a lot like piracy, well, it basically is. The difference between a privateer and a pirate is that letter of marque authorizing what they are doing.

One of the cool things about this is that here on Earth, in our history, we had people who had one of these letters that would basically absolve them of their actions, and they would sometimes get a letter of marque from two different countries like France and Spain. They would justify the attacks on Spanish ships with the letter of marque from France, and then do the exact opposite. This was illegal and, of course, they didn't tell either country that they were doing this. And, of course, some of them got caught and they were accused of being pirates and punished accordingly because they had violated the idea of being a privateer by playing two sides against each other. That sounds to me like a story waiting to happen.

Some countries also refused to recognize the letter of marque from their enemies, and then they would just hang the privateers as pirates. Sometimes they only threatened to do so as a way of extorting an exchange of prisoners or something else. Anything larger than a frigate was not typically used for this because it was considered unsuitable. So, therefore, there wouldn't be any ships-of-the-line being used as privateers.

SHIP SPEEDS

Time to talk about ship speeds. The first one we're going to talk about is when people are using oars because this is pretty straightforward. The top speed doesn't really matter because people can't keep that going for very long. If there is a favorable wind, a ship can do about two to three knots. With an unfavorable wind, it's about half of that, or one knot to one and a half knots. Earlier, I said that many of the wind-powered ships can reach 11 knots as their maximum speed, so you can see this is pretty slow by comparison.

And now comes the harder part, which is trying to figure out how fast ships can travel by sail. We should keep in mind that during a coastline-hugging trip, the ship will dock for the night in a port if it is able to. This is going to slow down the trip a little bit, of course, because they are not actually sailing for however many hours they are docked. By contrast, when sailing over the open ocean, a ship will have enough crew that they can sail continuously.

Now, I have some calculations that we're going to use. These are going to be kept relatively simple. These are also going to be done in miles. Speed is measured in knots. A knot is one nautical mile per hour. That means that a nautical mile is 1.151 land miles. If you're wondering why there's a difference, well, the nautical mile accounts for the curvature of the earth while the land mile does not. That's mostly a piece of trivia that you can surprise your friends with. What this really means for us is that if we've decided the distance between two ports on the coast is 25 miles apart by land, we would have to multiply that number by 1.151 to learn how many nautical miles it would be. In this case, that would be just under 29 miles. Whether we measure in miles or kilometers has no affect on the time that the trip takes.

Now, most ships have an overall speed of between four and six knots during a long voyage over the open water, but they're going to have about three to four knots during a coastal trip or along islands. Ships can go slower or faster than that, but they're not going to be able to maintain the ideal speed, or the maximum speed, of roughly 11 knots because of the variations in windspeed and direction.

If you want to figure out how long it takes to get somewhere by ship, here is how you would do this. The first thing you would do is measure the distance on your map, if you have one, using miles. Then divide that number by 1.151 to get the nautical miles. If the ship is going six knots, then you would take the nautical miles and divide that by six knots to get the number of hours of continuous sailing needed, meaning this is not taking into consideration any stops for the night.

Let's use an actual number. If we had 77 miles, we would divide that by 1.151 to get 67 nautical miles. Traveling at 6 knots, we would take the 67 nautical miles, divide that by 6 knots to get 11 hours of continuous sailing. At 4 knots, it would take 17 hours, and at 2 knots it would take 33.5 hours. So, it's not as hard as it seems.

WEAPONS INSTEAD OF THE CANNON

I do have a number of other subjects that are discussed in the book, *Creating Places*, but the last subject we're going to cover today in this podcast is the weaponry. If we have decided that there is no gunpowder, guns or cannons in our world, that means that the ships have no firepower. Therefore, there is really no drama to these. So, the question is what can we use as an alternative? Before we talk about that, we should probably understand what the cannon is, how it works and how many people are needed to fire that. So, let's take a closer look.

The largest cannon typically found on a ship in the Age of Sail is a 36-pounder, which means it fires a cannonball weighing 36 pounds. This cannon took 14 guys to operate. One of these people is a powder boy who goes and gets the gunpowder. This role is eliminated if we don't have cannons, of course. One thing this might mean is that if we have 100 cannons, then we might have 100 fewer crew because we don't need the 100 powder boys. Although, I do think that one powder boy could actually work on two different sides of the ship. But you get the basic idea that the number of crew might be reduced when we reduce the number of people needed to operate a weapon that is going to replace our cannon. We may not ever want to mention this, but it's something to keep in mind.

There's also a chief gunner who is responsible for priming the cannon for firing, but he's not actually the one who fires it. But this role is the one who is in charge of the crew. The rest of them are called gunners. There's a sequence that I describe in the book that I'm not going to go into here, but it basically involves prepping that cannon for firing, actually firing it, and then re-prepping it.

One issue with a cannon is that there is tremendous recoil, which means that the cannon flies backwards away from the edge of the ship; the hull. Therefore, it has to be forcibly moved back into position by all of these gunners. This is one of the reasons why there are so many crew for these really large cannons.

So, if we don't have a cannon, then what can we use? I can tell you that I did a lot of research and looking into this, and the only thing that I could really find that really makes since is the ballista, which is basically a giant crossbow. If you use something like a catapult, well, that has a motion that is going to interfere with the rigging because there's all those ropes holding down those sails. The ballista is one of the few things that has a firing motion that's similar to a cannon, and you could actually have it inside the hull. Granted, a ship might have to be built slightly different to accommodate one of them, but it still could fit in there and fire through a hole just like a cannon.

The big question here is how much firepower and range does that really have? The Roman ballista could fire over 500 yards and it was made of wood. But if were to make ours out of iron and have metal for the arms, this could give us greater power. We also might have a fictional alloy of greater strength, like adamantine, when that can provide even more power. Such a fictional alloy could produce a range that is greater than the Roman ballista. A

12-pounder cannon could fire 1,500 yards. While the practical range was a lot less, we can certainly claim something similar for our new ballista. Being plausible is the bar we need to get over.

Now, as far as firepower, a ballista is strong enough to fire straight through an armored knight and pin him to a living tree. We're talking about a real ballista, not the fictional one that we're going to invent. Obviously, one could blow a hole in the side of a ship, especially when the wood is not of a living tree because a living tree is much stronger wood than any wood that came from a tree. Now, in the book I go into some other details like how many people you might need to fire one of these, but I'm not going to cover that here. I'm also not going to cover how fast a ballista could fire, but I'm just giving you this basic idea of something that you could use to replace a cannon with. Either you can do some more research on your own, or you can pick up a copy of *Creating Places* and read what I came up with.

TRAVEL IN SPACE

Hello and welcome to *The Art of World Building Podcast*, episode number eighteen. Today's topic is travel in space. This includes the different types of engines, what to include inside a ship, and why we have a lot of freedom to decide how long it really takes to get anywhere. This material and more is discussed in chapter 9 of *Creating Places*, volume 2 in *The Art of World Building* book series.

ENGINE TYPES

It's fair to say that most of us have no experience traveling in space. The result is a need to do research on what this is really like. We can also rely on TV shows that we've seen, whether those are fictional in nature – and movies – or we can rely on TV shows that are more informational. Now, as it turns out, I work at NASA, but I am not a rocket scientist. But I do have access to people who are rocket scientists and I have run some of what I'm going to tell you by them to get their buy-off on this.

The first thing to talk about is propulsion because there are different kinds of engines that are used in space or in an atmosphere. Some of these are real and some are fictional. One thing I've noticed that's interesting is that if an engine type is real, authors don't typically spend the time explaining how it works, but if it's fictional, we do.

However, we don't really need to do that if we don't want to. I suspect one reason this happens is that authors have as little interest as the average person in explaining how an actual technology works, but when we've made up something interesting, we're trying to attract the attention of the audience as well and say, "Hey, wouldn't it be cool if this thing existed and it could do this? Here are some ideas on how that might work." And it's all speculative. Some science fiction makes a lot of mention of this, like in *Star Trek*, but others don't make any mention of it at all. So, you have a choice here. If you don't want to write a bunch of techno babble that you hear in *Star Trek*, then don't.

AIR-BREATHING ENGINES

So, the first kind of engine we'll talk about are the air-breathing ones. These are obviously designed for when there is an atmosphere. In other words, this is not in space where, obviously, there is no atmosphere. So, in an episode about travel in space, why am I talking about this? Well, because your ships might still have such engines. Now, with real technology, I don't explain in this podcast any more than in a story of mine how it actually works for the reasons I just mentioned. So, I'm not going to cover all the different types of air-breathing engines. We just need to decide if our spaceship has these.

Why would they? Well, arguably, space engines are designed for space. Therefore, they may have attributes that don't make them work quite as well in an atmosphere. Therefore, our ship may be able to alternate between these. When I watch certain science fiction shows and movies, I sometimes hear the pilot say something like, "Switching to so-and-so power," as they are changing from one type of maneuvering to another. Sometimes that means when they're going from space to an atmosphere or the opposite. This is a detail we can add to our ship to make it more believable.

Now, if we like the idea that we have ships that don't need this, we can still do that because, in any science fiction setting, just as today, we have different technology. Some of it is old and some of it is newer. So, we could have our characters on a ship that is old and, therefore, they have to do this kind of switching back and forth between air-breathing engines and space engines. We can have a character remark that he's making this change and say that this spaceship is a bit of a clunker because they still have to do this, and he prefers the one he doesn't have to make this kind of switch. Obviously, this is just subtle detail and not something critical to the plot, but such little details can make things more believable.

Besides, why have all of your ships be the same? This and other issues with their vessel could be the reason why they're on the lookout to acquire something better, which is certainly something that would add to your plot. They might want to steal something or buy something and not have the funds to do so, or someone might have stolen their ship and now the best they can do is afford this clunker. This issue of having to switch back and forth between engine types could be one of the things that this adds. Another issue with multiple types of engines is that they're probably going to have different fuel sources and, therefore, they could run out of fuel for one type of engine but not the other.

SPACE ENGINES

Let's talk about space engines. Space engines are divided into two categories: Those that allow faster-than-light speeds (or FTL) and those that do not, which are known as slower-than-light (or STL). Only the slower-than-light ones are real. Everything else is fictional. For slower-than-light engines, the propulsion is at least a little bit similar to atmospheric engines in that something is being ejected, usually from the rear of the vessel. This is, of course, what propels the ship forward. This is one reason why these types of engines could be used in atmospheric conditions instead of something that is specifically designed for atmospheric conditions.

Some STL engines could propel the ship fast enough that this can cause time dilation. This is when two observers experience a difference in how much time has passed. We sometimes see this in SF where the captain tells the pilot to travel a certain speed but not beyond a threshold because that's going to cause this time dilation. They may say, "Go up to speed eight, but no faster." Sometimes the captain will explain why, but really the pilot's going to understand already. So, sometimes, that kind of exposition is only being said for the sake of the audience.

One solution to that sort of scenario is to have an ignorant character standing there and ask the question, "Captain, if we're in such a hurry, why don't we go up to speed nine or ten when the ship can do that?" And have the captain explain why. We're so used to that kind of thing that we accept it, but if you stop and think about it, it's not that believable because anyone who lives in a society that has space travel is going to understand time dilation.

Here on Earth we do have space travel, but so few of us do that that most of us are only dimly aware of this. The only reason we've heard of it at all is from watching science fiction. But using the *Star Trek* example, in that sort of future where there is so much space travel going on, people are going to know this. We may need another solution, such as instead of the ignorant character, have someone else say, "Not in the mood for any time dilation today, Captain?" or something to that effect.

Let's take a look at some fictional faster-than-light drives, all of which are public domain, which means we can use these ideas.

JUMP DRIVE

One of them is called "jump drive." As the name implies, the ship can simply jump from one place to another one like it's being teleported there. As you can imagine, this is pretty convenient. What if you had a personal version of this right now and you could simply jump from home to work and back? While this is pretty cool, the problem that this creates for us as storytellers is that it pretty much eliminates all drama, tensions and problems that come with having to travel from one place to another. We're not going to run into enemy ships that are going to bother us unless we run into them when we arrive. We're not going to run across a distressed ship that needs help. In space, we don't really deal with monsters typically, but there's this issue of when you're traveling, stuff happens. Well, that's not going to happen in this scenario.

In that sense, there could be a lack of tension and, therefore, a lack of drama. And that's not necessarily a good thing. If you have this sort of drive, I would suggest using it sparingly in your setting so that this is something rare. It's also a little too easy for characters to get out of trouble with this if they're doing something and then enemy ships show up, they can simply jump right out of there. They're not going to have to fight unless the jump drive is malfunctioning or something. As you might expect, since there is no actual travel, a ship that has a jump drive is not going to experience time dilation when they use it.

Hyperdrive

Another type of drive is the hyperdrive, which is a drive that moves a ship into hyperspace. This is a fictional, separate dimension that is adjacent to normal space. Storytellers often use this idea that a ship that's in hyperspace has difficulty or it's not even possible to interact with a ship that's in normal space. One reason we do this is that hyperspace has some advantages and, therefore, we should also give it some disadvantages. The greatest advantage is the speed with which it allows a ship to travel great distances. This type of drive also experiences no time dilation when people return to normal space.

Warp Drive

That brings us to the last space engine, and that is warp drive. This is probably associated with *Star Trek* for many of us, but this is a public domain idea. There's this idea that there are different levels of warp, such as warp five being slower than warp six. The instantaneous travel, like jump drive, is not possible with warp. There is also no time dilation, but one of the issues here is that the ship is remaining in normal space. One thing that I don't see mentioned typically is that there are plenty of objects with which a ship can collide. Despite the word "space," there is a lot of stuff out there. It's just that it is fairly well spaced out.

My big point here is that a ship is not going to be traveling this fast unless it has some sort of shield to protect itself from that kind of debris. So, a believable detail we can add is that there's been some sort of battle and, as a result, the ship's shields are down and someone says, "Hey, we need to get out of here at warp drive," and someone else says, "Well, no. We can't do that because we could hit something." Having to leave that scene of the battle at a slower speed could also pose problems for them.

Distance Issues

Now we're going to look at distance. One of the realities of space is that any two locations are not going to be a fixed distance from each other. Everything is orbiting something. Moons orbit planets, planets orbit suns, and even the sun orbits the galaxy. All of that this means is that the distance between two places is always changing. In a previous episode about land travel, I talked about writing the words "not drawn to scale" on our map. Well, if we've created a map of a star system, we don't even need to do that because it's not going to be relevant. There's also the caveat that no one can show up and tell us that our fictional star system has things that are a different distance from each other than they really are. One impact of all of this is that two objects, like two planets, might be on the same side of the sun, or on opposite sides, or somewhere in between.

As you can imagine, this could significantly change the amount of time it takes to travel from one to the other. In some science fiction, authors make no mention of this, but in other stories, they do. The way we would typically want to do this is to basically say that the characters need to get from where they are now to another place, but maybe they don't have enough fuel to make the journey, given how far away that other location is at the moment. Maybe they have to wait a week or a month to do this. Or they could leave right now, but one of the issues is that it's going to take a month to get there when they need to get there in only two weeks, maybe because there is an event taking place on that location in two weeks. Someone could remark, "It's too bad that this didn't happen several months ago when the planets were closer."

This is also the sort of situation where if someone had a jump drive, it would be very advantageous because it wouldn't really matter. On the other hand, if they don't have it, then maybe they have to use hyperspace. Maybe they need to use slower-than-light travel, but they need to go beyond that threshold that's going to avoid time dilation. They're going to go so fast that they will cause time dilation and there's just no choice. They've got to do it. Mentioning this sort of detail or putting it into your storyline is one way to make things more believable. One good thing about all of this is that it gives us flexibility to inject this sort of problem into our story.

At times, we might want to make it suddenly very easy for the characters. Like two planets or locations happen to be relatively close and they're happy about that. Other times, we may want to make it more difficult. Try not to imagine that everything just works out magically and that there is no problem, ever.

Also bear in mind that when a ship is traveling to meet a planet, for example, it's not traveling to where that planet is now, but where that planet is going to be. Naturally, this sort of thing involves computers figuring out some of this math for us, but what if the computers are down? Can we have a character who is pretty good at this sort of thing doing it manually? They can at least start their journey based on the manual calculation. Then, if someone gets the computer working, they can input the fixes later. This is another way to be more believable.

One of the problems we could face is trying to figure out should we first create engines that can travel a certain speed and, therefore, cover a certain distance in a certain amount of time, and then base our story around that, or should we create our story idea first and then figure out what kind of engines we want to make available? That includes coming up with engines that don't quite do everything that our characters need. This is also one way to force them into a situation where they have a ship that doesn't do the job, but if they had a different ship, well, then that would take care of the problem, such as a ship that has jump drive. I would say that we should invent a propulsion system first and then alter how far away locations in our story are based on the needs.

External Ship Structure

One question we may face as world builders is what is the internal structure of our spacecraft? In a visual medium like television and film, we're also going to worry about the external view because we're going to have depictions of this on-screen. Now, most likely, if we are working in that sort of medium, we are going to have somebody who has designed that spacecraft for us, but for all I know you are the sort of person who depicts that spacecraft.

When it comes to the exterior of a ship, there is a tendency to draw something that is aerodynamic looking, even if it's designed to be in space. One notable exception to that is the Borg Cube from *Star Trek*. When it comes to these more aerodynamic ships, one of the reasons we do this is that this ship may have to operate within an atmosphere. Now, we may decide that the ship is never, under any circumstances, going to operate within an atmosphere, and therefore we can get away with something that is not aerodynamic. Otherwise, if we think there's any possibility it can enter an atmosphere and operate there, then we should make it aerodynamic. Any character who sees such a non-aerodynamic vessel is going to automatically assume it can't operate in an atmosphere.

But just because something is aerodynamic looking doesn't mean that it is designed for atmospheres. So, why would it still look that way? Well, just because we expect it. There is still the matter of slower-than-light propulsion ejecting matter, which is sometimes on the sides, but it could also, most likely, be on the rear. And then there's the reality of needing to look forward through a window, for example, at the space that you are traveling through. Both of these lend themselves to that similar ship shape.

However, when it comes to that window, we could dispense with the window and use a series of view screens instead. There are other issues like this that we can consider, but basically it doesn't have to be that way. It just can be. If we present it that way, the audience is never going to shrug and say, "Why in the world does it look like that?" We basically accept that without even thinking about it.

We may also want to consider where the ship can be loaded. On Earth, when you're getting on a cruise ship or anything else on the water, the cargo typically goes on the bottom, regardless of whether it's loaded from the back or the side. The reason for this is that we don't want to make the ship top-heavy so that it doesn't topple over. In space, we obviously don't have to worry about that. Unless there is artificial gravity, the cargo is not going to weigh anything. That kind of brings up another point. Why don't we ever see a cargo hold on a science fiction vessel where everything is basically floating? It's always shown as it is pulled down. It's just sitting there. The obvious answer for this is that it's easier for the film crew to film it that way rather than using special effects to show everything floating all the time. But it seems plausible that you would not want artificial gravity in the cargo hold.

Of course, this is going to depend on how the ship is generating that artificial gravity. If it's one of the more believable rotating vessels, then obviously everything has gravity and there's only so much you can do about that. However, on that note, if you do have a rotating vessel, there's going to be more gravity on the farthest reaches of that vessel than towards the center where there's still going to be almost none. Once again, this is something that is sometimes overlooked. It's a nice detail we can add for believability. Most of the living space would obviously be on the farthest reaches of that so it has the maximum gravity that they've intended for people to have. But there might be maintenance things that are happening towards the center of that vessel where those people have to float.

Now, if we don't have to worry about that cargo having a weight to it, we could assume, "Hey, it can be loaded anywhere." Well, what if people have done that and they've loaded all the cargo on, say, the left side of the ship, and then this space-faring vessel enters an atmosphere? Suddenly, it's going to have gravity and all that weight is going to be on one side. The next thing you know, our ship is lopsided and it might crash. Naturally, this is one scenario where maybe they do have artificial gravity in the cargo hold all the time so that they don't have to worry about this. But it could also be a situation where as they are preparing to enter an atmosphere, they have to go and turn on more artificial gravity there, or something to that effect. Maybe they also have to move the cargo around prior to this. If the cargo was loaded in space, maybe they didn't worry about this, but if the cargo was loaded on the ground where there is gravity, then they would have worried about this. But then, maybe once they're into space, they rearrange things.

There are some other considerations like where the weapons are located and where the engines really are, but we can basically make up a lot of that. The big thing we need to worry about there is that we don't want guns that can accidentally shoot into the ship. By the same token, we obviously don't want engines that are going to burn up part of the ship. What this really means is that the slower-than-light engines that are ejecting matter to cause propulsion are probably going to be on the sides or in the back, but really the faster-than-light engines with these fictional ways of getting around, we can pretty much put that anywhere. We might have a ship design where the slower-than-light engines are on a typical location that we would see on an atmospheric engine, but the faster-than-light ones, we could just decide to put that wherever we want. We could put that further inside the ship so that it is more protected from enemy fire.

INTERNAL SHIP STRUCTURE

Let's talk about the internal structure of our ship. If our ship is really small, so much so that only two people can fit inside it, for example, then the internal structure doesn't really matter because it's probably a single room. But if we're talking about something like the *Enterprise* from *Star Trek*, then the structure of the ship does matter. One reason is that characters need to move between locations, like the bridge, the cargo, the engine room, and their quarters. We may have active scenes such as aliens breaching the ship at a certain place in the hull, and it might be five minutes for our characters to get there at a full run, but they need to get there in two minutes because, otherwise, the aliens are going to destroy something.

To some extent, we could just make up scenarios like that, but if we're going to use the ship repeatedly, we may want to have a sense of this so we can be consistent. We don't want it to take five minutes to make that trip in one story and then two minutes in another and then ten minutes in a different one. Having planned out our ship to some degree helps us think of scenarios like this to start with. We can organize our vessel to avoid one problem, but we're probably going to set up another one. So, no ship is foolproof and any scenario could come up where it just causes a problem.

There are certain realities that are going to exist on a ship, such as the living quarters being somewhere near the dining areas. Now, that said, if you've ever been on a cruise ship, they do have the main dining area, but they have all sorts of smaller restaurants spread throughout the vessel. Such a scenario will also be true on a large spacecraft. Similarly, there will also be things like lounges in different locations so people can relax regardless of where they are.

Things like propulsion and cargo are located towards the rear of a vessel. More importantly, they are farther away from the living quarters because most people don't want to be near that, partly because that area tends to be a little bit on the dirty side. If you're creating a passenger ship, this is something to keep in mind. The cheaper rooms are going to be in such an area, or at least near that area.

If we do plan out our ship, I would suggest not going overly detailed unless it's really going to matter to your story. For example, you may want to say that engineering is on deck six towards the rear of the vessel, and it's on the port side, for example. You can just leave it at that. You don't have to say that adjacent to that is some other area. You can basically decide a certain deck and one side of the ship has a certain number of things, and not actually figure out exactly what is right across from each other or next to each other until it matters in your story. Being a little more generic and general about the location of these things gives us some flexibility if we need to change things later.

As for what we're going to include in our ship, we obviously need a bridge, which is the command center where all the decisions are being made and where a lot of the senior officers are during the important scenes. We're obviously also going to need to living quarters. Now, one thing that we may want to do there is have the officers have better quarters than the regular crew. Whether our ship is a passenger vessel or not, it's going to have a certain amount of entertainment. It's just that the number and type of those are going to vary. Even on a military ship, we're still going to have shops because people need to buy supplies. On a passenger ship, many of those shops are going to be concentrated in a mall-like area.

Any vessel could also have a jail, which is also called the brig. A military vessel is almost certainly going to have something like this, but even the passenger ones may have one. We may also want to plan out where the escape pods are if these are going to be used in our story. These are typically going to be mostly near the living quarters, but some of them are also going to be spaced throughout the ship so that those who are working the ship and controlling it when it needs to be evacuated still have somewhere to get to relatively quickly rather than having to go all the way back to their living quarters.

WHERE TO START

Finally, let's talk about where to start with space travel. The first decision we should really make when planning a vessel is to decide where it's going to operate: only in space or both in space and in atmospheric conditions? Another early decision: Is this a cargo ship, a passenger ship or a war vessel? In some cases, it could've started this life out as one thing and have been converted into another. We should also decide whether the purpose of our ship is local travel near the planet where it originated from or is it intended to go in between solar systems or even stars? This will determine what sort of engines are needed. If the local solar system is relatively peaceful, then it may also determine how many weapons it has. We should also figure out what kind of events we want to take place on this ship and what kind of vulnerabilities it might have which can be exploited by the way we layout the ship.

These are just suggestions. You can do things in whatever order you decide. One of the general recommendations I always make is if you have an idea for something, just work on that first. The best point of origin is an idea.

CREATING TIME AND HISTORY

Hello and welcome to *The Art of World Building Podcast*, episode number nineteen. Today's topic is about how to create time and history, including why we should usually keep timekeeping like minutes, hours, weeks, and more similar to Earth, and how to create historical events. This material and more is discussed in chapter 10 of *Creating Places*, volume 2 in *The Art of World Building* book series.

WHY CREATE HISTORY?

The first subject I want to address is why we should create history. The short answer is that it adds a certain believability and realism to our setting. And we don't have to go crazy with this. For a short story, we might not do any history. For something like an epic trilogy, we're almost certainly going to want to. Regardless, we don't have to do what Tolkien did and create an elaborate history. So, what are we really looking at?

Well, most of our stories are going to happen in a sovereign power, such as a kingdom. No kingdom stands alone. It's going to have other kingdoms that are friends and that are enemies, and these are going to have some history with each other. Our story might not take place in just one sovereign power, but in multiple ones as the characters move from one to another to do their quest, for example.

Some of this history is going to be relatively recent, like a war that happened in the last 100 years, and some of it's going to stretch back maybe 1,000 years. On a similar note, even within a single sovereign power, that form of government, as we've talked about in a previous episode, is not going to stay the same over the course of 1,000 years. It may, at one point, be a dictatorship which falls and then becomes a democracy, which also then falls later and becomes a federal republic. So, these things are always changing and each one of them leaves a mark on the sovereign power.

More specifically, it leaves a mark on the settlements there as far as building styles and other things that are left over from the past. It's also going to affect the minds of the people who live there and their attitudes about their own power and others. Some of that will depend on how recent this event was and how good the technology is. In a medieval-like society, people probably don't remember too much about what happened 1,000 years ago due to education. This is something to keep in mind. If we're going to create an event that happened 1,000 years ago in a medieval society, then people are only going to know the very basics of this, like there was a war, who won and maybe what it was fought over. They may know where it happened, partly because we sometimes name areas after a battle, and they might know a villain or a hero from that. And that's all they're really going to know.

So, when we're creating such an event, that's all we have to create. The great part is that this is relatively easy to do. Even so, we should only do it if it's going to somehow have an impact on the story that we're telling now.

One of the clichés that often comes up in fantasy is that there is a long-vanished civilization that has left a number of relics that our characters will discover and use. If we want to do such a thing, then we're going to have to think of at least a few events about the formation, demise and then what happened while that sovereign power existed. One of the ways we can use this is that we often have a quest or some sort of journey that our characters are taking through the wilderness, for example, and along the way they run into an overgrown civilization; a city that has been reclaimed by the weeds. This kind of thing is fairly common in Conan stories, for example. This is the sort of setting where some sort of monster or an artifact of some kind is lying around and ends up being picked up by our characters, and that unleashes some sort of problem or reawakens some ancient evil.

Now, we don't necessarily have to create the history for that, but it can be a good idea. This also depends on whether you're going to use that setting more than once. I have a planet called Llurien that I've been building for 30 years, and I plan on using for the rest of my career in addition to other worlds that I make up for whatever one-time use. So, if I do something like that in that setting, I need to know where that civilization came from and what was going on. I also need to know why it disappeared.

The reason for this is that if I don't work those things out and I later do something else in that area of the map, I may contradict myself. By the way, I think that doing this sort of thing is one of the advantages to having a main setting that you intend to use for a long time. I can create all sorts of backstory that I use repeatedly.

Earlier, I mentioned that in a fantasy setting people often don't know history, but if you think about it today, even with all the technology and information that we have, a lot of people don't know that much about recent history, or certainly ancient history. We will have heard of things, of course. Like, we all know who Napoleon was, but most of us don't know the details of this. This is something to consider. If you only know a little bit about Napoleon, like that he was the king and then emperor of France, and that he was involved in a certain number of wars, he was supposedly really short – which is actually a myth. He was basically the same height as everyone else around that time, but he was short compared to us today. You know, you only know a few basics about him.

So, do you need to create much more than that when you're creating a fictional history for some sovereign power of yours or a character from that sovereign power? I would say that the answer is usually no. The reason for this is that your characters are not going to know. You shouldn't be launching into a long exposition about somebody anyway.

What I'm getting at with a lot of this is that it is a good idea to quickly create some history. This is one of the easier and less in-depth things that we need to create as world builders. And yet, it can make our world seem like it goes far back in time. Which, of course, if it was a real world, it would. In post-apocalyptic fiction, we definitely need at least one major event – the one that caused that apocalypse. But, once again, people may have no real understanding of what actually happened, or any of the details leading up to this. One reason this is true is that it is the nature of an apocalypse that the technology tends to be wiped out. With it goes much of that written history.

I'm going to finish off this section with an example of a historical entry that I made up for the *Creating Places* book just to show you how short these entries can really be. The great thing about these is that they're so easy to create that we don't need to spend a lot of time on them and we can do them at any moment, really, and just insert them into our history file. So, here's the sample.

"Hessian 124. The Horn of Killian Lost. Legendary necromancer, Killian of the Lorefrost, suffers an ignoble defeat at the hands of Lord Sinius of the Kingdom Norin when Sinius kills a spectral knight who is in the act of blowing the Horn of Killian. The resulting vortex pulls all the souls into the horn, killing that of Killian, who briefly disappears from the world. By the time he returns weeks later, destroying Sinius, the horn has fallen into unknown hands."

So, what this gives me is a couple characters and an artifact that is lying around on my world that I could use. This can almost seem like a writing prompt in the sense that by writing one of these I can give myself a story idea, either about the past of those events I just described, or the present story where that horn is found and something bad starts to happen. But do you know something? This is a great way to generate ideas for stories. Even if you never write one, so what? You created a good historical entry. I sometimes just make up stuff like this and then, later, I find a way to incorporate that into a story.

SHOULD YOU CHANGE TIME MEASUREMENTS?

Let's talk about how time is measured on our invented world. If everything is Earthlike, we can basically ignore this subject, but if we want to do something a little bit different, then we need to think about how far we are going to go with that when it comes to making it different from Earth. Generally, I urge caution on this. If we alter the measurements too much, such as a day has 40 hours in it, and then we say 3 days has passed, that's a lot more time that's really passed on that world than what our reader is going to understand has passed. Even if we tell the reader that the days are 40 hours long, we might have to remind them because they're going to forget. There's this kind of mental inertia that takes over. People just assume that things are like here.

So, a general piece of advice is to keep things relatively close to the same. So, maybe a week that has six or eight days instead of seven, but not making a week have twelve days. But, of course, it really depends on how often you're going to mention how many weeks are passing. Weeks and months are arguably mentioned a little bit less than years, days or hours. In other words, we often talk about how old something is in number of years, and we often talk about how many minutes, hours or even days has passed since one event or another.

For whatever reason, at least in my experience as a reader and as a storyteller, I don't mention the number of weeks or months that have passed quite as often. The likely reason for this is that the story is taking place over weeks and months, and we're actually showing all of that time passing in smaller increments of minutes, hours and days. More to the point, we don't usually have nothing happen for weeks or months and then just pick up several weeks or months later and have to tell the audience how much time has passed. On the other hand, we do often mention how many minutes, hours and days have passed because it's more common for us to skip that amount of time and then have to inform the reader. So, let's focus a little bit here on minutes and hours.

I recommend leaving both minutes and hours basically the same. There are other ways to make our world different without messing with our audience's sense of how much time is passing. Now, it is true that on another planet, time will likely be measured differently, but the fact is our audience is here on Earth and they need to quickly understand time references in Earth terms.

Certainly, in science fiction, if the characters are from Earth and they're arriving somewhere else, even if time is measured differently on that place, they're still going to think of it in Earth terms. So, someone from that planet might say it's going to be an hour from now, and one of our Earth characters says, "Well, that's an hour and a half in our terms." The big question here is what do we really gain by doing something like that? I would say that we're only trying to create the sense of a different place. But there are many other ways to do this that don't mess with something so basic. Does our audience really care that time is being measured differently somewhere? I would say no.

Let's talk about days in the week. Of course, on Earth, we have seven. Most of us don't know why. The reason for it is that ancient civilizations were only able to observe seven bodies in the sky, and that includes the Sun and Moon. For whatever reason, they decided that that would be a good way of dividing up the weeks. That's where we get Sunday from, obviously. And, of course, Monday is really Moon day. Now, many of the planets are named after gods, and that's where we get Thursday from, which is actually named after Thor. So, that's really Thor's day.

We could choose to do the same thing on our invented world, or we could choose a different rationalization for naming the days and, of course, choosing how many days there are in a week. But I would still recommend going with something that's only off from Earth by a day, such as six days or eight days. This achieves our goal of making it seem like a different place from Earth, but it keeps it relatively similar. In other words, it doesn't have the side effect of messing with our audience's sense of time passing.

Bear in mind that people would have names for the days in your setting, and this is something that we should invent and occasionally have our characters use. The same way that if we were writing a story here on Earth and we had a character thinking about something that's going to happen next week, he might say, "Next Thursday I'm going to do so-and-so." Well, that kind of commentary is usually omitted from science fiction and fantasy books precisely because the world builder has not taken the time to name the days. One problem that this causes, though, is that people have no idea what those days mean. If Thursday is called "Lienday," and I have a character mention that, the reader here on Earth is going to have no idea how far in the future that is. So, we're going to have to do a little bit of explanation. I talk about that more in the book, and there are some simple tricks we can use to make that easier.

We can also determine the number of weeks in a month. As it turns out here on Earth, this is not set. Instead, it is the number of days in a month that determines how the weeks are laid out. We often have four full weeks, but we seldom have five full weeks. We often have a four-and-a-half week situation going on in a month. We could choose to standardize this, and that might be a good approach because it keeps things consistent for our audience so we only have to say it once and it's probably going to be a little easier to remember. On the other hand, if we do something like we've done here on Earth where it keeps changing every month, that's actually pretty confusing. The only reason we understand that is that we live here. This is one thing that we probably do want to change.

When it comes to the months in a year, we once again want to stay to something in the range of 11 to 13 so that it's only 1 month off from here on Earth. We should, once again, name these months because our characters are going to refer to them. Our naming convention may want to follow something similar to Earth where we use the suffix "-ber" or "-uary," – such as January, February, December, November – to add this to the month's names. Now, we don't want to be completely consistent, just like we are not completely consistent here on Earth, but by having two, maybe three of these, and using those two or three consistently, we get a certain amount of inconsistent and consistency that it gives people the impression that we've put some thought into this, and so have the people of the world. One point I'm making is that too much uniformity can seem too much like we planned it out.

UNIVERSAL CALENDARS

The next subject I want to touch on is the universal calendar. In our modern world, the Gregorian calendar is accepted worldwide, but this wasn't always true. In many countries, they still have their own calendar and they only use ours when they're working on things that are worldwide. There are pros and cons to doing a universal calendar, so let's talk about some of the benefits first.

A universal calendar helps us reconcile differences between two dates. So, if we say that it's 734 D.C. in Kingdom X, and that's 30 years later than 343 O.E. in Kingdom Y, well, that's kind of hard to figure out what's going on. We need a way to reconcile this, at least in our notes. Especially in fantasy, each sovereign power may have its own time measurement. Year 1 is going to be something important, like the year that the kingdom formed. On Earth, the birth of Christ is what's used, but this was not recognized for hundreds of years, and didn't become standard for several hundred years after that. So, if we're trying to find a universal date for the whole world, this can be a little bit difficult. We would need to have an event that impacted everyone, or was at least recognized by everyone. A mass exodus from a planet in science fiction is one way to do that, and some sort of cataclysm is another way.

Now, there are some challenges that come with a universal calendar. If we decide to use month names that have something to do with a season, we have to remember that in the northern hemisphere, when it's winter, it's going to be summer in the southern hemisphere. So, something like that needs to be avoided. In addition, if we call it something like "Snowtime," obviously that's going to be different in each hemisphere. But at the equator, there isn't any snow. This is a mistake I made a long time ago. So, learn from my mistake. Don't do this. That's really the only major challenge to this is coming up with the month names. So, this is a pretty easy subject.

WORLD HISTORY AND EVENT TYPES

When we're trying to fill out our world's history, there are some categories for these historical events. So, let's just go through some of these one by one. The first category are events involving the gods, which of course is only going to come up if we have them in our setting. In some story worlds, the gods keep to themselves, but in others they interfere with life and cause events to take place.

For example, they could father children that are members of species or just monsters, demigods or whatever we want to call them. There might be sacred places that were built and then later destroyed and these could be significant events. They might also have magic items, like Cupid's bow or Thor's hammer, and these could fall into the wrong hands at some point in history. Using Cupid's bow as an example, maybe a mortal got a hold of this and shot somebody with it and that person fell in love with another person and this caused some sort of event to happen. If you've created magic items for the gods, this is one of the great uses we have for those. It's arguably no fun if the gods never lose their items.

And then there's one of the biggest events, which is a god being killed or somehow incapacitated so he cannot influence the world anymore. As with all events in history, these may have anniversaries associated with them. Then there are technological events which is especially useful in science fiction. These can include missions that either failed or succeeded, and then there are launches of rockets, satellites or new ships. There could be discoveries. There could be weapons tests. A big one is first contact with other species and aliens. As usual, we don't have to say too much about these. Just note when it happened, how long ago, what month of the year, and what took place. This is true of all of the events we're talking about, not just the technological ones.

Then there are the supernatural events, which certainly comes up in fantasy, but also in science fiction. There can be phenomena that spring into existence or which are discovered. There can also be magic that can be discovered or expanded upon, or maybe it's squashed in one area of a sovereign power, whereas in another one it proliferates and becomes more popular and more used. Some of this can be the result of an event. It could be caused by a character of ours. There can be famous practitioners of magic, and there can also be famous victims of it.

Then there are the magic items that can be invented, lost or used in some dramatic way. Then there's the rise and fall of sovereign powers. Since this shapes not only the world, but history, this is certainly something that we should spend time inventing. Many of these kingdoms will collapse due to war, and this is another major event category. One thing we should think about this is what goal are we hoping to achieve? For example, maybe we want two characters from different sovereign powers to have animosity toward each other, and a war is one way to do this.

Now, there are usually things that lead to war, such as cultural differences, and that can also be a reason why they have an attitude towards each other. But there's no reason not to have that boil over into war either recently or farther in the past. It's especially easy to create wars between something like a dictatorship and a democracy because the ideology is so different. Another thing to consider is that two kingdoms that are friends today could've been enemies 100 or 500 years ago. Some other reasons for wars are things like taking back territory or trying to acquire resources that are in another sovereign power's territory.

Another category of events is groups forming, such as the Justice League from comics. When did this occur? There may be a special naval force, group of knights, spectral groups, or any elite guards, horsemen, archers or whatever other groups we've created. We should figure out how old these groups are. Sometimes there is prestige in being the oldest knighthood, for example.

Another category is missions undertaken to do something like explore, rescue, maybe kill or kidnap someone or something, or maybe to investigate a strange phenomenon. For all of these, we can decide when it happened and exactly what happened and what the result of this was. Especially doing this with a mind toward how does this impact our current setting or story? Some of the people who undertook such missions might be famous, either because they succeeded or because they failed, maybe in spectacular fashion. Such a person could be a cautionary tale and result in a world figure. We talked about creating those in a previous episode.

WHERE TO START

We're going to end here with a short section on where to start. History is great because it can be created at random. The short entries that we're going to write into a history file can be made up at any time. That said, we will sometimes want to focus on a specific subject and create multiple entries, such as the rise and fall of one kingdom. This allows us to get into a frame of mind about that subject. For example, earlier in this episode, I was talking about this fiction Horn of Killian that I made up. I could do other entries about that, such as when it gets found, then when it gets used in some dramatic way, and then figure out what its current status is. Maybe it's currently under guard.

So, we can create multiple entries about this, three or four of them, at the same time. We should spread out these events throughout our history so that we don't have four about, let's say, the Horn of Killian in a row. But in between each of those entries, we have other entries about other things. With so many things that we create, we try to do things in an order. But the great thing about history is that we can make it up in random order.

For something like that Horn of Killian, we can start with an event for when it was used, but we can go back and later create something about when it was created. It's less like writing a story and more like outlining one where we have freedom to go back and forth. Start with whatever you have an idea for and what you can use in your story. And if you make up things that don't end up being used, that's fine. You've still helped flesh out your world.

Creating historical events is one of my favorite things to do because there's so little overhead and weight to this in the sense that it doesn't really matter too much if we create something we don't use or if we change our minds later. This is one of those things that we could spend five minutes on here, and then not do anything with it for three months, and then spend another five minutes on it. I consider this one of the more lightweight and fun things to invent in world building.

CREATING PLACES OF INTEREST

Hello and welcome to *The Art of World Building Podcast*, episode number twenty. Today's topic is about how to create places of interest, including catacombs, interstellar sites, ruins, monuments, and more. Learn how easy these are to create and how they can improve interest in your setting and story. This material and more is discussed in chapter 11 of *Creating Places*, volume 2 in *The Art of World Building* book series.

ORDINARY PLACES

By "places of interest," I of course, mean somewhere that your characters are going to visit or hear about, and where something interesting has already happened or is going to happen to them while they are there. They may know that something interesting is going on there or they may be en route from one place to another and they run across this place and something is going on. For anyone doing a story that's action and adventure, this is something that we often need. If our characters are not traveling and they're not in an interesting location to begin with, then maybe we don't need to worry about this. But, for many of us, we're going to need this. So, let's look at some of these, and I want to start with some of the more ordinary places, for lack of a better word.

The first one I'll mention is catacombs and hidden passages. This can also include things like bomb shelters, sewer lines, tunnels and subway lines. Hidden passages can also be anywhere in a city or even in just a building. These places by themselves may not be that spectacular, which is why I said they're kind of ordinary, but sometimes we can place something spectacular inside them, such as a creature or a monster of some kind. They can also be used to interesting effect if a character is able to access one of these and get from one place to another without anyone realizing that they are doing so. We have all seen that kind of thing done in various stories.

There can also be lost items or items that were purposefully placed there, hidden there, and then, of course, somebody finds them and makes use of it, and havoc ensues. Another idea we've probably all seen is some sort of creature inhabiting these places and it uses it as a home or a base from which it emerges and then does unspeakable things that have been capturing people's attention, and maybe the authorities are looking into this. They eventually track this creature back to this lair. This has been done so often that it's something of a cliché, but if it's done well it can be really cool.

Another thing we can do is a map that shows these places, and people didn't realize that something was there, or the extent of them. Or maybe there's a room that's not on the map and this causes some intrigue.

When inventing such places, it's usually a good idea to have some idea why they exist. This is something that we will want to reveal to the audience at some point. Even early on in the story, if we have approached it in such a way that this place is supposedly ordinary, as I've said, but then, as it turns out, other things are going on there that had made it extraordinary. In other words, sometimes it starts off ordinary, and then something else happens that makes it more interesting. Of course, we don't need an elaborate reason for something like a bomb shelter, sewer lines or subway lines because it's kind of obvious. And even catacombs, where the dead are buried, have a certain purpose to it.

Where we need to think of a reason is something like a tunnel or a secret passageway. And we can keep that reason relatively simple if we just decide that maybe the occupant of that home, if that's where the tunnel is, was someone who is paranoid, or maybe they were, at some point, a robber baron or something where they were trying to smuggle stuff, hide it and not get caught. And, of course, we could decide that there is a nefarious reason for it all along, such as this is someone who wanted to murder people or kidnap them, and this is the place where they held those people.

Some locations may be military in origin, such as a place where some sort of secret research was being done. This is especially useful in science fiction. We can invent all sorts of phenomena that may not be supernatural but are something we don't typically see here on Earth, or are something that we just made up, and where that was being used for experiments, or maybe it was something that needed to be dug out of the ground and processed somewhere, and that's what the facility's origin is.

A mundane reason for tunnels could be something like excessive heat in tropical locations where people have created tunnels so that they can cool off during the day. This is obviously something for a less advance civilization because, even our civilization, we have air conditioning, so we don't need to do something like that. Now, such tunnels for that purpose could still exist because that could've been from 1,000 years ago when air conditioning, for example, did not exist. The idea of ancient tunnels and some sort of ancient evil within them is a fairly standard cliché, but again, if we use it well, it can turn out good.

If we have a world with dwarves or another species that is known for tunneling underground, then we don't need any special explanation unless we want to figure out why they tunneled into this particular location. The obvious answer would be to access something underground such as gold.

The last point I'll make about this is that sometimes these underground places are not known because they were created so long ago and, over the years, civilization has been built on top of them. And, as a result, modern people may not know, or at least very few people in the settlement may actually know that these are there. So, only a few people might be making use of them, whether that is for good or evil.

STEP WELLS

Now, I want to switch topics to something known as a stepwell. If you've never heard of these, I would Google the phrase, "Step wells in India," and you will see some really interesting pictures. Basically, what these are, instead of the typical well that we might see in the United States where it's just a kind of circular hole in the ground with a certain amount of brick wall around it on the surface, these are wells that are really large. I mean, they could be as big as a building. The reason they're called stepwells is that you can literally walk your way down the steps into the deep recesses of this well. This is something that can not only be used for drinking water, but sometimes people used to do their laundry in such a place. These were so big that people would often gather in it. Some of them look like an amphitheater, almost, the way they steps are all around in concentric circles, or usually in a square or rectangular configuration.

When I first saw some of these pictures, I noticed that, sometimes, a certain number of feet down into this stepwell there would be an opening that led into an underground area. And, of course, that immediately sparks the imagination about what could be in there. Another good use for this is that if you have a water-dwelling species, that species might actually be found there and, in fact, this could be the opening to a home of theirs or a place where the underground species and those on land get together and meet because that's the easiest way to get to these guys if they live in underground rivers, for example. I would take a look at some of these pictures, and maybe they will inspire your imagination the same way they inspired mine.

Monuments

Another area that we just touched on that we should also talk about are monuments like statues, buildings and monoliths. Some of these are going to be kind of ordinary, but some of them will be kind of spectacular. One of the reasons for that could be the size. If most statues are about 10-20 feet tall, and then there's one that's 500 feet tall, naturally, people are going to think that this is amazing. Sometimes it's the person who is depicted in something like a statue that makes it famous. We already talked about creating world figures in a previous episode, so this is one of the ways you can use these guys.

If we're creating a monument, sometimes these are celebrating an occasion like the end of a war, for example. So, we might want to think about why this thing exists. We can keep it simple. Another good reason is the foundation of the kingdom, for example. In another episode, we had also talked about creating history and events, and this is one way that we can use those again. We should also consider what condition these monuments are currently in, and how old they are because that will help us determine that. There's a long tradition of badly worn and somewhat forgotten relics of a previous age. Sometimes these are overgrown and being reclaimed by nature. This can add a certain spookiness to them. Monuments that are buildings might house things that are considered valuable, and therefore they may be prone to people trying to steal things or to desecrating them if they are also religious in nature.

Now, why would someone desecrate a religious place? Well, if they are someone who worships in another religion or if that place has been conquered by a foreign power. Sometimes these monuments are still standing, despite the fact that they are somewhat ruined. Any discussion of this sort of thing would be incomplete if we didn't talk about something like Egypt's Great Pyramids, the Great Wall of China, Stonehenge, or even the Seven Wonders of the World. Well, those are really the Seven Wonders of the Ancient World, and they included a temple, two statues, the pyramids, of course, and then a mausoleum, garden and a lighthouse.

Many of these were considered amazing architectural feats, so that's one of the reasons why they were considered amazing. In a world with a lot of technology, like in scientific fiction, it might be a little harder to think of something like this. After all, the most advanced technologies are usually something that we are featuring in our story, such as a spaceship, for example. So, something that's amazing on an architectural level may be simply dwarfed in coolness by something like a spaceship. Unless, of course, the spaceship is that thing, but then we're not really talking about a monument, are we?

By the way, if you're wondering why there are considered to be seven ancient wonders, that's because, back then, there were seven bodies up in the sky. That included the sun, the moon and then the five planets that had been discovered at that time. This is actually the same reason why we have seven days in a week. So, if you're looking for a different number of wonders in your world, well, you can do the same thing. If you decide there are six or eight heavenly bodies, then you can have six or eight wonders of your world. In science fiction, maybe it's something like galaxies or nebula that we are counting.

GRAVES

The last relatively ordinary place I'll mention is graves. Sometimes we have a mausoleum which can be enormous or uniquely decorated, or it could have someone famous buried inside it. Of course, this offers a good opportunity for grave robbing. Some of these might have guards, which could be ordinary or extraordinary, such as a ferocious animal, a monster, maybe a demon, something technological or even magical. So, if we have characters who are trying to rob this place, there's a lot of pretty cool stuff that we could put in their way.

Extraordinary Places

Let's talk about a few more extraordinary places. The first on my list is underwater settlements. This makes a lot of sense if you have a species that, of course, lives underwater. Why treat them like fish who are seemingly just migrating all the time, or who might use a coral reef as somewhere to hover around? We could actually have them building actual homes and settlements underwater. And these could be in various places. They could be actually at a coral reef or they could be created out of a cliff or something like an underwater mountain. In a setting with magic or technology, we could also decide that they have created this using that magic or technology so that there are places that have even pockets of no water inside the settlement so that visitors like humans can visit and be comfortable in a space that has been carved out for just them.

We could also use magic or technological portals that allow people to simply appear there and then leave. In other words, maybe they don't actually have to swim there or use a submarine or something to that effect.

A similar idea is the floating settlement. There are two versions of this. One is floating on water, and then the other one is floating in the sky. Unless the physics of your world are different, such as in the Avatar films where there are actually things floating for whatever reason, we're going to need magic or technology to achieve the effect of something floating in the sky. The great thing about that not being natural is that this can, of course, be sabotaged by someone and cause a major problem. As you might expect, whatever is holding it aloft is going to be under heavy guard to prevent exactly that kind of catastrophe.

Aside from the fact that this place is floating in the air, it may not differ from other places by that much. However, there are a few ways in which it is different. Obviously, you can't just go wherever you want by walking off the edge of this, unless falling to your death is something that you really want. All kidding aside, that does suggest that the ends of this place are not only heavily guarded, but it might actually be impossible for you to walk off the edge. Of course, you don't really need the edge. You could fall down something like that famous scene from one of the *Star Wars* films where, right when Darth Vader tells Luke Skywalker, "I am your father," he falls through that chute. The next thing you know, he's hanging on the bottom of this floating city and he's about to fall to his death. Except, of course, somebody comes by and rescues him. So, there could be other ways within the city that you could end up falling through the bottom.

On that note, that scene may not be particularly realistic because you would think that they would have some way to detect that there's a heat signature on something, and maybe they should try to rescue whatever's down there. Another issue that we should think about is that most likely the only danger to this place, aside from a malfunction that would cause it to crash to the ground, is going to be being attacked by something that can fly. In SF, we have ships that can attack this place, but there may be natural creatures like dragons that would exist in a fantasy setting, where they can also pose a threat. But all of those threats that might be on the ground, they're not going to be able to do much. One of the problems that we might have is that doing any sort of trade with this place could be an issue. In fact, any sort of farming is typically done outside the confines of a settlement, but if it's up in the clouds, what you going to do for food? You're probably going to have to get it from somewhere else. Then the question becomes, how do you get it here? There are some logistical things that you may want to think about. These can add some interest to your setting.

Another concern is, what do you do when there are hurricanes or other strong storms? What kind of protection does such a place have from these? When it comes to realism, this is the single most realistic reason not to do floating settlements at all, unless we're talking about a world where the weather is pretty much always calm.

Now when it comes to settlements that are floating on the water, we actually do have one of those called Venice here on Earth. However, it's kind of an illusion. Most of the city I actually on stilts, but it gives the impression of floating on water. But since we are writing fantasy or SF, we can get away with one that actually is floating on the water. Once again, a water-dwelling species is the likely culprit behind creating such a place, or being very prominent there.

But as we were just talking about a minute ago, what happens where there's a storm? Something that's built underwater doesn't experience this that much because it's insulated from the effect of even a hurricane, especially if it's deep enough, like a hundred feet down. But anything on the surface is obviously going to be pretty affected by waves. Now when it comes to Venice, it's protected for the most part by a lagoon. If you're thinking about creating such a place, you might want to think about putting a natural protection around it like that. Or it can be artificial, and once again, something can go wrong with that protection.

Another issue is, of course, the sea monster. This could affect both floating settlements and those underwater. If those monsters are known to be around, maybe these settlements don't exist at all. They may provide too easy a target for something like this.

STRANGE PHENOMENA

Another kind of place of interest that we can create is one where there are strange phenomena. This is something of a staple in both fantasy and science fiction. Space offers the possibility for nebulas, radiation and even alien planet environments. Strange planets offer all sorts of possibilities that we can make up or base on something that NASA has discovered. One of the great things about space phenomena is that we can basically have them be wherever we decide to put one.

By contrast, any sort of weird phenomena that's on a planet or another body, like a moon or an asteroid, is typically associated with a given location and it isn't going anywhere. This means that while it can be discovered, it also could've previously been discovered and it is already known to be in that location. This, in turn, could mean that people are going there on purpose to make use of it in some way. How will, of course, depend on what the phenomena is. Making it something dangerous is often particularly attractive to us. This can be true, even if the phenomena could have a positive result such as being able to harvest something from it that can be used in a positive way, such as powering a space engine or, possibly, providing a cure for something. Just because it can be used for good doesn't mean that something bad cannot happen when people are trying to collect it, or if they just encounter it by accident.

Speaking of accidents, that's a really good way to create phenomena. We can have either magical disasters or technological ones. Having an explanation for a phenomenon is optional. Sometimes it will improve things, and other times we might want to just leave it a mystery. Sometimes we can actually do both and just leave it undecided for a long time, and then, eventually, someone figures out where this phenomenon originated. Experiments gone wrong, or especially a battle where something has happened, such as a ship being destroyed, are good sources of such phenomena. We can also use these phenomena to create monsters or other creatures who have come in contact with it, and possibly been transformed in some way. This is where superheroes in comics often originate.

While we're on the subject of space, let's talk a little bit about meteors. These can, of course, impact a planet and leave a crater that a less technologically advanced people might wonder what caused this, and they may assume that one of the gods did something. People can also attribute something supernatural to a meteor that is seen passing through the sky. This can be true if that meteor comes by at regular intervals, such as every 25 years, or if it's only a one-time occurrence. Now, in science fiction, people probably realize more what's going on, and they may not have this kind of myth anymore. But, even so, such an advanced civilization, or people from that, could be traveling around and come upon a planet where the technology is much less advanced. And, as a result, the people there do see this as something spectacular.

EVENT SITES

While we're on the subject, we also have event sites. And the meteor crash could be one of these, but there are others such as a famous battle happening somewhere, or maybe the tide of war turning. Or there could be something like a species that was massacred somewhere, or maybe there was just a really high body count. Now, all of the examples I just gave are kind of gruesome, but we can create other positive ones as well. For example, there could be a place where a prophet revealed something, such as the way Moses is believed to have brought down the Ten Commandments. We also have things like a shrine, a church or a monument that may mark a special site that has a positive association. The monument could be somewhere where something happened for the first time, such as magic being discovered, or a type of magic, or something like the first contact with an alien species, or the first launch of a technology.

There are also natural phenomena like the Aurora Borealis, geysers or even sinkholes that sometimes gain special significance. Some of these places are a little bit more ordinary than some of the others we've been talking about, but we can make them more interesting by associating them with a cool story.

Ruins

Another type of area that we've touched on before is the ruin. These can be a bit of cliché, especially in fantasy, but these are places that are ripe for death by misadventure. We can have monsters there, treasure and other items that can lure people there, for one reason or another, including something like a distress call that is going out. Some ruins will be legendary, and some of them will be unknown and discovered by accident by our characters. Danger is often assumed to be in these places, at least if we are setting a story there, because otherwise what's the point of having our characters run across it?

Audiences tend to enjoy watching people explore a place and wonder what's going to happen next. One twist we can do is having our characters not be the first ones who have run across it, but maybe someone else just did so the day before and they are still present. And now we've got a bit of an issue going on between these two different groups of characters.

A good ruin is like a mystery where, as a storyteller, we slowly unfold the story of what's going on now, and maybe where this ruin came from before. And one of the ways to do that is to place interesting places within this. You know, we're talking about creating places of interest. Well, the overall ruin can be a place of interest, but within there we can create some of the things that we've already talked about, such as monuments. The trick is to figure out how we can have our characters discover multiple things of interest where the general interest of this place is continuing to rise as they interact with it. We may also want to figure out what happened to the people who used to live here. One of the obvious examples is simply that they were attacked, they were conquered, and then this place became abandoned. A more mundane reason is something like trade routes drying up or the local economy falling apart.

Now, no one typically does that kind of thing in stories because it's not that interesting, even though that is a major reason why some places become ruins. It's arguably better to have an interesting reason behind it being discovered than something kind of boring like this. We should also figure out how overgrown this location is. A rainforest or a swamp is going to quickly consume a place so that it's almost impossible to find. On the other hand, a desert is only going to slightly bury the place.

LAST THOUGHTS

Now, one of the subjects that I'm not going to cover today is shipwrecks and what we can do with these to make them interesting, and that includes the reasons they are famous. I'm also not going to talk too much about where to start with creating places of interest because they are relatively easy to do and it's one of the things that we can create kind of on the spur of the moment when we are not in the midst of creating a story or something that's more involved like a species. This is a kind of lightweight thing that we can just create, and we might even create some things that we don't use in a particular setting any time soon, or we just create it in general and then, maybe one day, we're creating a setting and we go, "I had this idea. Let me take that and put it in this setting because I now know how I can use that."

So, this is a great way to just invent stuff on the fly. Spend 10 minutes here, a week later you do another maybe 30 minutes of working on an idea, and you can just accumulate really interesting things that you can eventually find a use for.

CREATING MAPS

Hello and welcome to *The Art of World Building Podcast*, episode number twenty-one. Today's topic is about how to create maps like continents, settlements, and dungeon maps, and learn whether you should create any of this and why. This material and more is discussed in bonus chapter 12 of *Creating Places*, volume 2 in *The Art of World Building* book series

ADVANTAGES TO MAP MAKING

There are some advantages to creating a map. One of those is that it makes it easier for our audience to visualize locations. That can, in turn, cut down on how much explanation we have to do about which direction various things lie in. That does not free us from acquiring the skill to quickly and succinctly describe the various locations of things, but, even so, it can take some of the pressure off of us. Personally, I find myself describing things in too much detail when there is not a map. But when there is, I feel comfortable able just staying, "This kingdom is south of the other one, and next to this feature, like a forest or an ocean." I know that the reader can flip to the map and just see exactly what I'm talking about. And there are various other details that I don't need to go into if they are not relevant to the passage that I'm currently describing.

There is a tendency to try to describe a complete setting. The problem with this is that we're just doing a paragraph of explanation. Depending on who you ask, that kind of exposition is not considered good style, but you may disagree and just go ahead and do it anyway. But it is still worth mentioning that cutting down on some of that explanation can be a good idea. As they say, a picture is worth a thousand words.

For world builders, another really good reason to create a map is that when we have these blank areas on the page, it can help us think of things to include there. As authors, we're all familiar with the idea of a blank page keeping us from thinking of anything, but that's a little different when we're talking about writing. When it comes to creating a map, it's a little bit easier to think of things to place somewhere.

One of the general tips that I'm going to give you today is to base your maps on something that already exists on Earth, but also make alterations to that. For example, I, personally, have trouble thinking of interesting city layouts. I just draw a blank on this, if you'll excuse the pun. So, one of the ways of getting around that is to use a program like Google Maps where you can just pull this up, focus on any given city, town or whatever, look at it and think, "Do I like the layout that I see here? Is there something that I want to borrow?"

Many people are not going to recognize it if you take that existing place and you create a map that looks very similar because most of us don't look down on the place where we live, or even other places nearby, or ones that we're very familiar with, from that vantage point and really pay attention to the layout and the way it looks from above. We typically know what it looks like more from the skyline, or just what it's like to live there, not from above. But if you're going to choose a place that's extremely well known, like Manhattan, then yes, you probably want to switch it around a little more.

And this is very easy to do. You can just change the direction of things. So, let's say that you have an island that is mostly north to south. You can just turn that to face a different direction. You can do the same thing with countries. If you model one on France, people are going to recognize it if it's exactly the same. But if you turn it sideways, they may not. And, of course, the other thing that we can do, and probably should do, when we do this is to make more changes to it while we're doing so. We can just chop off a whole section of it, add on another section, or maybe there's something that we'd like from another region of the world and we want to add that to this continent or this region that we've created. It's an easy way to alter that without having to generate something from scratch.

The same idea applies to any settlement map that we come up with. All we have to do is alter a few parts of it and no one's going to recognize it. Many of us don't have drawing skills, and we think of that as a negative when it comes to creating maps, but this is actually a way that this is a positive. Because if you could duplicate it exactly, well then, that's going to be recognizable. If you can't duplicate it anyway because you don't have the skills like me, then that's good because it's going to look different and that's what you want. So, some of us might think of taking out tracing paper to trace it exactly. I would say don't do that. Just do it free-hand and see how close you come or what you feel like altering.

The thing about the shapes of countries and settlements is that they're very specific. If it's recognizable at all, there is something distinctive about it. So, all we have to do is change that. And we're talking about even a minor amount of change can make it unrecognizable.

What I started to touch on earlier is that one of the advantages to making maps is that it can help us think of things to put there. If, for example, you draw a north to south running line and decide that one side is ocean and the other side is the continent, and then you put a city right in the middle of that continent/coast edge, now you're going to be wondering, "Well, what else is near this? Do I have a mountain range? Do I have a forest? Is there a river right there? So, there's a tendency to want to fill up the map. The problem that we sometimes have is what do we put there? So, it becomes an issue of making decisions.

One easy way to get around that is to do what I was just talking about, which is basing it on something from Earth. But the other way is to understand some basics about how land regions form and things like prevailing winds and rain shadows, which we've talked about in a previous episode, but I'm going to briefly touch on that again here.

One of the points I want to make about this subject is that it actually makes it much easier to decide where to place vegetation once you understand it. So, rather than it being a burden to you and something like you feel like, "Now I have to get things right when I'm creating a map," the reality is that once you understand this, this is actually going to make a lot of your decisions for you. Now, you're still going to have artistic license, or you can kind of overrule things or play with the details to get what you want, but it solves that problem of the blank page where you're looking at it and you go, "I have no idea what to put where and how any of this works."

Well, once you understand how it works, it becomes really easy to think of where to place things. Since this is a podcast and I can't show you an image, which would be worth a thousand words, I'm going to come up with a very simple explanation for you. For example, let's say that we have a coastline that is running north to south. On the left of that is the ocean and on the right is going to be our continent. One of the things that's likely to happen is that we could have a mountain range that is also running north to south. Or, in other words, it's parallel to the coast. A good example of this, if you have a computer with you, is to look at a map of the west coast of the United States.

So, let's say we've got our coastline and then, maybe two inches to the right of that, we've got this north/south mountain range. Let's go ahead and decide that this mountain range is 10,000 feet tall. That's the average height of the mountains. If you're wondering why that matters, it will become more apparent in a moment. But what's basically going to happen is that the winds, in our example, are going to be coming from the left side of this map and crossing over that mountain range. The higher that mountain range is, the higher the atmosphere is going to be pushed up and the more rain is going to fall. As you'll see, this is going to cause some vegetation issues.

Let's say, for the sake of argument, that our continent is located roughly where the United States is. That means that the prevailing winds are coming from the west, or from the left side of this image that we have in our head. In other words, all of the storms are going to be coming from the left, and they're going to be passing over the right. This also means they're going to pass over that mountain range. What is most likely going to happen is that we are going to have a bunch of lush vegetation, like a forest, in between this coastline and the mountain range. This is being caused by the prevailing wind and the location of this continent on our hemisphere on our planet. Basically, this is a certain number of degrees north of the equator. As a result, that's why the winds are coming from the left or the west.

Now, once those winds pass over the top of these 10,000-foot-tall mountains that are running north to south, most of the rain has fallen out of those clouds, and, as a result, there is no rain, or very little rain, to fall on the right side of those mountains. The result is going to be a desert. This phenomenon is called a rain shadow. Now, further to the right of this desert, as the clouds continue to move, they're going to pick up some moisture in the air because that's just the way it works. There's always going to be some. It's just that most of the moisture is picked up over the ocean.

So, what's going to happen is as these prevailing winds move further and further away to the right of this mountain range, they're going to pick up a little bit more moisture, and more of that is going to fall. So, what's going to happen is that desert is going to give way to a grassland on the right. At first, it's going to be short grass and then it's going to be taller grass. That's going to give away to a savannah a little further to the right. A savannah is mostly grass, but more and more trees coming in. And then, even further to the right, eventually we're going to end up with more forest because enough rain is falling that far away that this rain shadow effect has decreased.

This is a pretty simple and believable example. And, to some extent, it is based on the United States. If you look at a map of the U.S., you do see this. You see lush vegetation on the west coast, then you see the mountains to the right. Further to the right, you see some deserts, like Death Valley. Further to the right, you get the Great Plains. And then even further, you finally start getting more forest. However, this kind of process, it plays out across the Earth, and it would happen on any Earth-like planet that you have.

Let's briefly talk about another scenario. We were already talking about this north to south running mountains. Well, what if they weren't north to south but they were east to west? Well, basically, that's not going to have any impact because the winds are blowing to the right and the mountains are also laid out in that direction. Therefore, the mountains are not going to be blocking anything. You could have plenty of rainfall north and south of this mountain range that is east to west.

This is something to consider. One way that you might use this when creating a map is that if you really want, let's say, a really thick forest that stretches for 1,000 miles on this side of the continent, and you also want mountains, then don't put the mountains facing north to south. You're going to have to put them east to west. So, this is something you probably want to know before you draw those mountains on your map.

There are a lot more details like this that are included in the *Creating Places* book. So, if you really want to get into this, I recommend picking up a copy. Most of it really is not that hard. You just have to read about it. One of the goals I had in writing that book is that I collected a lot of that knowledge in one place for you when I did the research on the various scenarios that come up. Now, one thing about this is that we still have artistic license and we can still decide that things are slightly different for one reason or another, and we can also decide that there's magic at play, or other phenomenon that don't happen here on Earth. But, generally, we probably want to try to be realistic if we are creating a place that is roughly Earth-like.

HOW TO CREATE
CONTINENT MAPS

When it comes to continents, one thing that I find happens is that, as I'm drawing out a map, I start to think of the different kingdoms, and reasons for conflict among them. This is a really good reason to create one, even if you don't include it in your book. For example, I could have a forest that is capable of producing the right kind of wood needed to build ships. Perhaps this forest is inside one kingdom and, therefore, another one that is adjacent is unable to get into it without cooperation. They're either going to have to work something out or they're going to have to go to war. Now, you might not think that wood for ships is a good enough reason, but there could be a lot of other things. And, even when it comes to ships, that can really control who can be a seafaring power. And, as we probably know from the way the Earth is right now, one of the reasons Britain was able to get so far around the world and dominate so much, and why culture from Britain is all over the place, is that they had one of the greatest, if not the greatest, navy at the time.

But it doesn't have to be that. It could be any kind of mineral, something like gold, or any other precious metal that is inside one kingdom but is not in the other. Or we could have decided that it is a situation where part of that mountain or forest is in two different kingdoms, and therefore it has always been in contention.

Another scenario that came up for me was that I once created a continent, that you can see on my Llurien.com site called "Llorus." There is a sea that's called, I think, "The Sea of Fire." Basically, the opening to the sea is on the left side of the continent. So, if you picture this, you've got a coast that's running north to south, and then there's an opening into this sea, which is kind of like the Mediterranean if you want to use an Earth example.

One thing I decided to do, and which is obvious, is that one kingdom was in control of the land to the north of that opening, and a different kingdom was in charge of the land that is to the south of that opening. Naturally, both of them want to control access to that sea. Therefore, both of them are seafaring powers and their ships are frequently spotted, both in the ocean and in that channel that leads to the sea. And, of course, in the sea itself.

This set them up as enemies for each other. Now, as it turns out, inside that sea, there are multiple other kingdoms that have an access point to that water. They might also like to be able to sail on that sea. And, more importantly, they might like to be able to sail out of that sea and into the ocean, but doing so requires them to either get past the ships of both of those other countries, or to be an ally of one or the other so that they can get through safely.

One of the things that this allowed me to do was begin establishing friends and enemies. Now, as it turns out, I had done a lot of research into different kinds of government forms, and that's also included in the *Creating Places* book. But, you know, ideologically, there are different ways of looking at the world, and different governments form as a result of that.

Sometimes, countries are opposed to each other for ideological reasons. I sometimes begin setting up the enemies partly because of that and partly because of where they were on the map. Once you have a certain amount of knowledge about various things, you can begin leveraging that knowledge when you are doing world building. That is, of course, the whole reason why I wrote *The Art of World Building* book series. In fact, if you really want some good examples of this, I believe the first chapter of *Creat-*

ing Places is called "Case Studies" or something to that affect. I basically showed you how you can use this
knowledge in the act of creating a setting.

Now, as far as whether you should draw one or not,
one of the reasons not to is that if your characters are not
going to be traveling through the wilderness, from one
place to another, like an epic quest like you would typically
see in something like *The Lord of the Rings*, then you don't
necessarily need a map. On the other hand, the farther
they're going to go, the more helpful it is for both you and
the audience to have one of these. If your characters are
from a lot of different places, they've been brought together and there are cultural clashes and other things, and you
keep referring to those various regions or kingdoms, people can become very interested in getting a better idea of
where everything is in relation to each other. They might
want a map.

Now, in a previous episode, Episodes 15 and 17, I
talked about travel on land and on the water. In both cases,
the ability to come up with believable time frames is
helped by a map. But, on the other hand, the map can also
constrain us a little bit if we feel like we've drawn it to
scale, which is something that I encourage people not to
do. It can help us and it can also be a hindrance, so you
have to decide how much you want to worry about that.
Personally, I find it to be very helpful because it helps me
avoid making unrealistic estimates about how long someone's going to take to get from one place to another. Just as
importantly, it helps me avoid contradicting myself. This
obviously matters more on a world that you intend to use
repeatedly than one that you're only going to use for a
short story or just one novel.

One of the things I like to recommend to people is that
you do create one world that you go more in-depth on and
you plan to use for the rest of your career. And then, for

the rest of the time you're writing, you just create a setting for the particular story that you're going to use. This gives you the best of both worlds as far as creating a lot of stuff that's very detailed, for one, and then just kind of doing one-off stuff for another.

I also want to mention that you don't have to create the entire continent map. You can just do the region that your story's going to take place in. However, I do recommend that you have at least a rough idea of the other things that would affect that local region.

For example, figure out how far from the equator that area is. Figure out if there is a mountain range to cause a rain shadow to happen. Just getting an idea for these kind of things is good. And you don't have to draw them. You can just indicate, "Okay. There's a mountain range off to the left. That's where the ocean is. The equator is 400 miles to the south. Therefore, the prevailing winds are coming from the left." Just kind of come up with some general parameters, even if you don't draw them on the map.

One of the other pluses to map-making when it comes to continents is that if you do understand things like climate zones, as we discussed in a previous episode, it will basically decide for you where your climates are. That can help you figure out what kind of clothing people are typically wearing. Again, one of the biggest problems in world building is that you have so many decisions to make and we often can't think of a reason to make one. Well, some of those decisions can be essentially made for us. If that sounds too restrictive, well, we still have creative latitude. That pun was actually not intended.

GETTING STARTED
WITH MAP MAKING

Now, there are a lot of programs that you can use to create maps. The process is basically the same regardless of what you use. The tool only determines some of the details of how you actually place things on the map. I happen to use a program called "Campaign Cartographer" which comes from Pro Fantasy. They have an optional add-on called "Fractal Terrains," and I use this to generate a continent shape pretty quickly. You can just click a button and it gives you a new one. Or you can use some of the other techniques that I talked about in here, such as taking parts of existing continents and alerting them, flipping them around or even combining them with other continents. Once I have a shape that I like, I will pull that into Campaign Cartographer and then use the landmass tool, I think it's called, to draw the shape of my continent over the top of that, and then hide the background image that I used as a source. My inability to draw is not a problem because I'm trying not to get it exactly the same anyway.

Once I've done this, I'm going to decide how far away from the equator this place is, and which hemisphere it is in if it's only in one. This will tell me the direction of the prevailing winds. Once I do that, I can start drawing mountain ranges with an eye for what kind of affect that's going to have on vegetation. That is the basic process that I suggest people follow.

After that, the details are a question of artistic imagination. Campaign Cartographer comes with different color icons for different settlements, such as blue, gold or red. I tend to use that to depict all of the settlements that are in a given kingdom. This is one way that I use to indicate where one kingdom ends and another begins. One of the great things about that particular program is that you can create pretty large maps, and all you have to do is zoom out. And if you want a more regional map, you just zoom in more and you can just take a screenshot of that and use that with your book. And it does produce images that are professional quality. I have published those in many of the books, including the *Creating Places* book that we're talking about here, when I made the examples for this book.

If you don't think you have the skills, or maybe not the time or interest in acquiring them, you can certainly hire people to create maps for you, but you're still going to probably need to at least describe what places look like, where they are and what life is like there to give people who are going to draw your map for you some idea of what to work from. But I would recommend learning how to do this because it's fun and it really does spur the imagination.

How to Create Settlement Maps

When it comes to settlements, these are included in books less often. One problem I have found with trying to do a settlement map is that you only plan to use a few of the buildings in that settlement, and yet you're going to have to draw so many of them. Once again, the challenge becomes how do you decide what to put where? This is one reason to base your settlement on something from Earth.

But another thing we can do is create something like an area that is considered old town. This is the area where this settlement first existed and, at one point in time, that was the entire town. Usually, this is going to form around or near the source of water. So, that's one way to make this decision. Another way to get started is to figure out where a castle or similar fortification stands. Then we can start building outward from there.

Now, the idea of using an old town only works if this is a larger settlement, like a city, or if it's an especially large town. If it's a small town, then old town is the entirety of the town in most cases. Even so, you can still use the principle of starting where the water source is. I, personally, don't usually create a settlement map, partly because I do have trouble envisioning that. But what I often do is, as I write the story, I start to have a mental image of how things are laid out, and that can actually help me. So, in that sense, I ended up doing it kind of backwards. What do I mean? Well, I start working on the story, or at least the plot of the story, and that helps me form the map in my head. I sometimes then start creating the actual map, fleshing out what I've pictured.

One reason to go ahead and draw the map, even if it's coming after the fact, is that if you ever return to using the setting again, you won't have to read your own book to understand where everything stands. I have this problem with a book I wrote about a decade ago where there was a pretty specific layout. I'm going to have to return to that book and my only way to know where everything is is to read my own book again. Of course, I'm going to do that anyway, but I might have to do it just to understand the layout. That particular city also had a really specific layout where it was important and it mattered to the plot where everything was. So, that is the kind of situation where you may want to create a settlement map.

Something else to keep in mind is the concept of zoning. What that means is that you've got commercial, industrial and, usually, residential areas. The residential areas are obviously where people live. The commercial is going to be all the stores. Those are typically near where people live and near the industrial areas. And, of course, the industrial is stuff like factories. One of the big decisions to make is that you want to keep the factories away from the living areas because factories typically smell, to keep it simple. Obviously, people don't want that kind of pollution near where they live. This concept of zoning is something that can help you plan out a settlement on the large scale so that you have an understanding of what is where. Depending on the technological level of your settlement, it may make sense — and this often happens — where the industry is sometimes placed near the water. So, if you've got a river or a port, that tends to be where the industry is. If you've got a nice, little forest, or maybe a hill, that tends to be where residences will be. Then, of course, a hill is where something like a castle might be built upon.

I find that it's helpful to just have a general sense of where the rich people live and where the poor people live if they are segregated like that, and then where industry and residences are. Just kind of come up with a high-level idea before you start worrying about placing buildings.

Something you may also want to consider is whether you have multiple species there and if they are segregated at all. For example, elves tend to prefer trees, so there might be an area of your settlement that is heavily forested — maybe not heavily, but it at least has more trees, more parks, and that might be the area where the elves tend to live. If you had a species like dwarves where they often tunnel underground, you may have a castle that's built on a cliff and the dwarves are allowed to build tunnels into those cliffs and have some of their homes there.

HOW TO CREATE DUNGEON MAPS

The last subject I'll talk about briefly is dungeon and ship maps. These are something that we don't typically see with books, but certainly come up with gaming. There is something about any sort of underground labyrinth that, for me as a reader, seems inherently confusing. I often don't understand where the characters are in relation to where they were before. Even as an author, when I am trying to plan out what's going to happen, once again, I often have trouble figuring out why does any corridor go this way or that way, or end up in this room, and what is that room for? In my story, the reason that room exists is that maybe I want them to be attacked there, but that room should have an actual purpose that the people who invented or created that place had for it. This can be even more difficult for us to figure out than why everything in a city is where it is.

Now, if you've ever worked as a janitor or a field like that where you are typically in the bowels of a building, you may have some better understanding of what's going on with things like boiler rooms and other facilities that are required to operate that building in an efficient manner and in a comfortable manner for its occupants. Those are the kinds of functions that are most likely going to be going on in an underground area.

Of course, another one of these is the dungeon. When creating a dungeon, you may want to think about how something like a prison is laid out. I haven't looked into this, but I would image that an abandoned prison, like Alcatraz, might have maps online where you can get a feel for how this place is laid out because it's no longer in use, and therefore there's not as much of a secret. When a prison is being used, obviously the inmates shouldn't know all of the nooks and crannies of this place. So, a map of a currently used prison may not be available, but we can probably find one for an abandoned one to get some sense of the layout of such a place.

But one thing that immediately comes to mind for me is that most buildings don't have these long hallways that go off into various tangents and there's no rooms on either side of them. Every time there's a hallway, there's always a room immediately on each side of every square feet of these hallways. By contrast, it so often seems that in fantasy in particular there is some sort of underground hallway that's going for a certain distance, and then it just branches, seemingly at random, at some location. And then that hallway also branches again. Eventually, here and there, they find little rooms. This sort of thing seems to be based on something like the Pyramids from Egypt where the impression is that these hallways do this kind of thing. But, even then, I don't think that's accurate because if you look at the schematics for some of these pyramids, there are very few passages inside them.

The point I'm trying to get at with any sort of underground area or dungeon map is to make it a believable space that was once used and which is now abandoned. Try not to create hallways that go off in seemingly random directions and there's no rhyme or reason for them.

How to Create Ship Maps

Now, when it comes to ship maps, there are kind of two kinds here. There's the wooden ships, like the man-o-war, and then there's the space ship. For a wooden ship, there are pictures online, and even on artofworldbuilding.com where I have some links to this, where you can see the internal structure of a wooden ship. While it's not a map, it does show you where everything is located. It can be a good idea, if you're going to really use the interior of a ship, to take a look at one of these maps and just use that as your source. The average person has not seen one of these and they really don't understand it, so you don't have to make up something so much as you can leverage the way ships are actually built.

When it comes to spaceships that you are inventing, I think it's a good idea to have at least a rough understanding of each deck of that ship and what is there on the port side, on the aft side, on the starboard side and at the front of the ship. One reason for this is that you're going to want to be consistent when you have your characters travel from one area of that ship to another for a specific purpose, such as going from the bridge to engineering because something is going on in engineering. You don't want to say it takes 10 minutes at one part of your book, and then, in another book you're using that same ship in, now it takes 15 minutes to get there.

Having a map can also make it easier to decide that one side of the ship was impacted during a battle and, as a result, there are certain functions of that ship that have been compromised. You can, of course, make up that sort of thing on the fly, but that can lead us to doing things that are too convenient, such as deciding that all the food replicators have gone offline because that's what your story needs. Well, if you've already decided that those are on the right side of the ship, and engineering was also on the right side of the ship, you can also decide that there was some sort of damage to engineering. But if we haven't already decided that, we're not going to think of collateral damage that might make it more believable.

In other words, when planning damage to a ship, try not to have the damage only cause the exact impact that you need for your story. There could be other impacts that don't really drive the plot, but which are believable

Appendix

This appendix includes sections found in most episodes.

Review

If you're enjoying the podcast, please rate and review the show at artofworldbuilding.com/review. Reviews really are critical to encouraging more people to listen to a show haven't heard of before, and it can also help the show rank better, allowing more people to discover it. Again that URL is artofworldbuilding.com/review.

Subscribe

So, let's talk about how to subscribe to this podcast. A podcast is a free, downloadable audio show that enables you to learn while you're on the go. To subscribe to my podcast for free, you'll need an app to listen to the show from.

For iPhone, iPad, and iPod listeners, grab your phone or device and go to the iTunes Store and search for *The Art of World Building*. This will help you to download the free podcast app, which is produced by Apple, and then subscribe to the show from within that app. Every time I produce a new episode, you'll get it downloaded right onto your device.

For Android listeners, you can download the Stitcher radio app, and search for *The Art of World Building*.

This only needs to be done once and at that point, you will never miss an episode.

MORE RESOURCES

Let's take a quick break here and talk about where you can get more useful world building resources. Artofworldbuilding.com has most of what you need. This includes links to more podcasts like this one. You can also find more information on all three volumes of *The Art of World Building* series. Much of the content of those books is available on the website for free.

And the thing that you might find most useful is that by signing up for the newsletter, you can download the free templates that are included with each volume of *The Art of World Building* series, whether you have bought the books or not. All you need to do is join the newsletter. You can do this by going to artofworldbuilding.com/newsletter. Sign up today and you will get your free templates, and you will never miss an update about what is happening in the great world of world building.

More books are available in the series, including two workbooks, all at Amazon: https://amzn.to/3y7mN1B

Patreon Support

For those of you who support crowdfunding, I am on the patreon site and would appreciate any support you can lend. Think about whether you're benefiting from this podcast or *The Art of World Building* blog and website, and consider supporting the effort to spread the word far and wide. Your support could help a budding world builder create an awesome world that you become a huge fan of. This podcast and related items are my way of giving back to the fantasy, sci-fi, movie, and gaming industries that I love so much. You can give back too by helping to fund this effort. When the next Tolkien or George R.R. Martin shows up, you can tell yourself, "I helped him do that!"

Your support can be just $1 a month to the cause. Higher levels of support get you increasingly cool things, such as PDF transcripts of this podcast, free mp3s (including unreleased music), free eBooks and short stories, bookmarks, and even signed copies of books and CDs of my music. Many of these are unavailable to the public.

Just go to artofworldbuilding.com/patreon. You can also just go to the home page and click the big icon for this. Support great world building today!

World Building University

If you'd like to learn world building skills through instruction, I've launched World Building University. There you can find one free course you can take just by signing up, which has no obligation. Other courses are in development and available now. You can preview parts of every course, all of which include video lessons, quizzes, assignments, and sometimes downloadable templates that are even better than those found in the books.

To get your first free course, just go to worldbuilding.university.

CLOSING

All of this show's music is actually courtesy of yours truly, as I'm also a musician. The theme song is the title track from my *Some Things Are Better Left Unsaid* album. You can hear more songs at RandyEllefson.com. Check out artofworldbuilding.com for free templates to help with your world building. And please rate and review the show in iTunes. Thanks for listening

ABOUT THE AUTHOR

Randy Ellefson has written fantasy fiction for decades and is an avid world builder, having spent three decades creating Llurien. He has a Bachelor of Music in classical guitar but has always been more of a rocker, having released several albums and earned endorsements from music companies. He's an IT professional in the Washington D.C. suburbs. He loves spending time with his son and daughter when not writing, making music, or playing golf.

Connect with me online

http://www.RandyEllefson.com
http://twitter.com/RandyEllefson
http://facebook.com/RandyEllefsonAuthor

If you like this book, please help others enjoy it.

Lend it. Please share this book with others.
Recommend it. Please recommend it to friends, family, reader groups, and discussion boards
Review it. Please review the book at Goodreads and the vendor where you bought it.

JOIN THE RANDY ELLEFSON NEWSLETTER!

Subscribers receive a FREE book, discounts, exclusive bonus scenes, and the latest updates!

www.ficiton.randyellefson.com/newsletter

Randy Ellefson Books

Talon Stormbringer

Talon is a sword-wielding adventurer who has been a thief, pirate, knight, king, and more in his far-ranging life.

The Ever Fiend
The Screaming Moragul

www.fiction.randyellefson.com/talonstormbringer

The Dragon Gate Series

Four unqualified Earth friends are magically summoned to complete quests on other worlds, unless they break the cycle – or die trying.

Volume 1: *The Dragon Gate*
Volume 2: *The Light Bringer*
Volume 3: *The Silver-Tongued Rogue*
Volume 4: *The Dragon Slayer*
Volume 5: *The Majestic Magus*

www.fiction.randyellefson.com/dragon-gate-series/

The Ascension Quest Series

When Max awakens in the VRMMORPG game Llurien Online, he doesn't know how he got there or why he can't logout. And a Life Counter no other player has is steadily descending to zero. Can he escape before he dies?

Death Singer

www.fiction.randyellefson.com/ascension-quest-litrpg-series

THE ART OF WORLD BUILDING

This is a multi-volume guide for authors, screenwriters, gamers, and hobbyists to build more immersive, believable worlds fans will love.

Volume 1: *Creating Life*
Volume 2: *Creating Places*
Volume 3: *Cultures and Beyond*
Volume 4: *Creating Life: The Podcast Transcripts*
Volume 5: *Creating Places: The Podcast Transcripts*
Volume 6: *Cultures and Beyond: The Podcast Transcripts*
185 Tips on World Building
3000 World Building Prompts
The Complete Art of World Building
The Art of the World Building Workbook: Fantasy Edition
The Art of the World Building Workbook: Sci-Fi Edition

Visit www.artofworldbuilding.com for details.

Randy Ellefson Music

Instrumental Guitar

Randy has released three albums of hard rock/metal instrumentals, one classical guitar album, and an all-acoustic album. Visit http://www.music.randyellefson.com for more information, streaming media, videos, and free mp3s.

2004: The Firebard
2007: Some Things Are Better Left Unsaid
2010: Serenade of Strings
2010: The Lost Art
2013: Now Weaponized!
2014: The Firebard (re-release)

www.ingramcontent.com/pod-product-compliance
Lightning Source LLC
Chambersburg PA
CBHW031118020426
42333CB00012B/130